Our
Educational System
Flipped Upside Down

*Teaching Reading to Reduce the Negative Effects of School
Closures during the Pandemic, and Beyond*

"I WRITE SO YOU CAN TEACH SO THEY CAN READ!"

Barbara Stotts Cochran

ISBN 978-1-63844-232-5 (paperback)
ISBN 978-1-63844-233-2 (digital)

Christian Faith Publishing, Inc.
832 Park Avenue
Meadville, PA 16335
www.christianfaithpublishing.com

Printed in the United States of America

This book is dedicated to my husband, Malcolm, who supported my determination to complete my bachelor's degree and then encouraged me to earn my master's degree. Through his devoted interaction with our children from birth, I realized the true potential children possess and, if nurtured, the boundless levels of accomplishments they can achieve!

Acknowledgments

I thank my children, grandchildren, and children-in-law for the help and encouragement in everything I attempt!

I want to give special recognition to my daughter, Debra, for the beautiful illustrations which make the book more visually pleasing. Those drawings provide the focus that allows levels who are unaware that print has meaning to engage in creating the necessary foundation for future successes.

My grandson, Grant Bullock, Editor in Chief of Reading Teacher, LLC, did the nearly impossible with his patience as I crafted this book from its beginning through its daily revisions and editing. He and my granddaughter, Hannah, my most efficient discerning listener, offered constructive critiques to help me see the strengths and needs of my endeavors through objective eyes.

Barbara Stotts Cochran

Preface

The first six years of my formal education were in a one room country school where I was the only one in my class. One teacher taught all students from kindergarten through eighth grade. During my years there, I was not defined by, nor confined to, my chronological age or my grade-level attainment. Due to low enrollment, my country school closed, and I rode the bus to "town school." I became "another member" in my classmates' room which averaged twenty-eight students. The individualized benefits I enjoyed in the smaller population were no longer available. In retrospect, this early experience greatly influenced the structure I developed for my own students in my classroom.

I formed small groups of varying abilities, based on similar strengths and similar needs, for teaching the skills and strategies needed by those individual students. I also used that same structure in Title I classes and, later, in at-risk classrooms. Students were individually moved from one group to another as they mastered skills necessary to succeed at the next level. All reading *and* writing instruction was through trade books from my own classroom library or from our school library. Prior to the introduction of trade books as the vehicle for teaching all reading/language arts skills, I taught students in grade-leveled basal books with workbooks and worksheets. I also taught reading through content-area textbooks (social studies, science, and math). That genre requires a different approach due to the technical vocabulary which is more uncommon in learners' background vocabulary. The text structure is quite different as well.

To ensure that the needs of those individuals who were far beyond their chronological level and before schools were efficient in providing additional opportunities beyond their regular classroom, I provided research opportunities. In the early years before computer access, encyclopedias and other print were used. This necessitated reading instruction in those genres as well.

I was a stay-at-home mom for thirteen years when I had the priceless opportunity of learning, first hand, about child development in all senses of the concept. My husband, a school psychologist, who actually became my excellent mentor, and I have raised four children, who also became my outstanding instructors. All four have advanced college degrees. Of our six grandchildren, two have college degrees, two are in college, and two are in high school. Those six help me in reducing the generation gap and keeping me "in touch."

I have a bachelor's degree in elementary education with a reading endorsement and a master's degree in reading. I taught for twenty-seven years in classroom education, including Title I, K-5; first through sixth grades, departmentalized, where I taught all of the reading/language arts to multiple grade levels; first through fifth grades were, during some years, self-contained, where I taught all grade-level subject matter; and seventh through twelfth grades, at-risk reading/language arts classes.

I have taught gifted students and struggling students, and every level of attainment in between, at all grade levels.

I was asked to represent our school district at the state-level development of Language Arts/ Social Studies Portfolio Assessment of students' academic work. I was also asked to write curriculum for the school district by which I was employed and then facilitate that curriculum for colleagues. All of those experiences have added to the insights which are beneficial in this endeavor. Over the course of forty years of formal teaching, I have also tutored learners of a variety of ages and needs— some requested by the classroom teacher of record and some at the request of parents. I voluntarily tutored, after contract hours, those individuals from my own classroom when a normal school day did not provide the time necessary to meet the needs of some of the more difficult challenges for the learner *and* the teacher! I cannot say enough about how *much* the supportive attitude, both toward their child and me, that parents provided toward the success of their learners!

I will add here, as a veteran teacher, that it is *not always* easy to solve the learning issues with all students! It is *imperative* that students, parents, and teachers work together to provide the best possible learning experience for academic success for all *ages* and *abilities*!

I have substitute taught for thirteen years since my retirement, in classrooms of preschool through eighth grade, in multiple school districts. I believe "the best way to teach reading is through reading!"

Introduction

These books are written for the *providers* to gain insights into working with their learners for the most success in bridging any gaps caused by the school closures due to the pandemic. The providers' section, *Teaching Reading during a Pandemic*, offers the information that should be mastered before attempting to work with their learners. If it is necessary to search for the concepts needed when working through the "ABCs," the learners can become distracted and lose interest in the focus. If that happens, it will be *much* more difficult for them to become convinced that this is a helpful venture. I recommend that the "ABCs" be read for the same reason. It is difficult, even for seasoned educators, to present new information for the greatest effect without first familiarizing themselves with the information.

The embedded book, *The ABCs: A Collection of Collective Nouns for Animals,* is the *learners'* book. This book was written for providers to use to lead learners through the experiences to improve their skills.

These two combined books are written for very *broad* levels of *background experience* and formal knowledge on the part of the providers as well as the learners. Because I have no idea who will compose the audience for these books, I have used the ranges demonstrated to me during my forty-plus years in the teaching profession. Some of you may even be experienced teachers looking for more ideas about how to serve your population. *Some* of you may have completed the *minimum* requirements for public education. Some of you who are in the *provider* description may *also* find that you are part of the *learner* group and that you will gain missing elements in your own skills while working with your learners. I hope that I will meet *all* extremes in trying to improve the language arts skills in achieving success for each learner. I have tried to use common language throughout, but if you have a need to "look up" any words that I have used, do not be afraid to let your learner see you do that! I always kept a dictionary on my desk and used it any time I needed information. What better way to show learners that we *all* need to *use* what we teach them to do!

You will find that there are some repetitions in my books. They are indicators that the provider and the learner should continue their awareness of the noted material in any settings, including school-related assignments/requirements. Stimulation to reach beyond what is included in my books can be instilled in the learner to follow their own curiosities by some of the questions I have suggested. Those questions can be adapted to ANY learning situation, including school-related work. This book is intended to be supplemental, not just a stand-alone, one-use learning experience.

I have offered some suggestions throughout my books, not only to catch up on educational opportunities voided by school closures and the reluctance of some to reopen but also to move forward from where *each individual* is stabilized in their learning. It is my hope that these books will also offer valuable insights for those of you who are homeschooling. *All learners* have "gaps" for whatever reasons, perhaps illness when skills were being taught, or just not "tuned in that day." Perhaps something was just a bit too advanced at that point in time. Regardless of the reasons, my books are designed to address multiple needs.

You will find that the books which I am creating are *not* leveled books. They are *not* intended for *only one level* of learner. The vocabulary and concepts reflect my efforts to accommodate that *range* of learners and providers. It is expected that no one, other than an accomplished reader, can successfully gain all the information that is contained within, independently. My reasoning for this format is based on the reality that some families have more than one child and that those children will have different strengths and needs. This can occur even when the siblings are twins! It can be cost prohibitive for a family with such varied needs to equally acquire help for each learner. Also, *each* learner will advance through the various opportunities and still need help during the growing spiral of learning which I have interwoven. The same text can be used to address more advanced needs as well. Rereading the material and mastering it in different depths of understanding can give learners a foundation to begin seeking their own learning experiences about other subjects. This in-depth mastery also enables that learner to intervene positively with their inner circle of other needful learners.

Entries *A* through *M* in the *Collective Noun* book have a somewhat more controlled vocabulary and sentence structure. However, there is information to be gleaned by those who are more independent with reading skills in those pages. Also, the higher-level questions that I pose will likely provide new perspectives for many of those learners and their previous thought processes.

Entries *N* through *Z* are written without the controls and provide a more advanced "jumping-off point" for the more accomplished learner to also benefit from many of the skills and strategies that I offer. The more evolving capabilities of the novice readers can find these pages beneficial as well. The provider will need to read much of the information for the learner and fill in or use different terms for the earlier levels of understanding. Share these pages with that group of learners much like I explain in the (0) and (1) levels of activities. Although many skills are in place, there is some vocabulary and sentence structure that will need provider intervention.

Again, I strongly suggest that the provider *should read* through this *entire document* as well as the "ABCs" section before *ever* attempting to use it with learners. The familiarity that develops will lend to the fluent use and the trust by the learners that the provider is knowledgeable of the material.

With the suggestions in this book, I believe that all learners can benefit with minimal expense. A different book does not always have to be purchased for each individual. If modifications are made and realistic expectations for the book's use are set before the learner begins each personal experience, there is no reason that many levels of development cannot benefit from this and future books that I will produce. The books that you already have in your personal libraries, as well as school or public libraries, and any accessible school textbooks can, and should, be used in conjunction with "provider" information

Black-and-white drawings of individual animals provide excellent visual representation for the appearance of each animal.

Suggested Additional Purchases to Use with These Embedded Books

* spiral notebook, minimum of 70-page count with wide lines
* color matched plastic 3-ring flexible binder with one-inch rings
* 3 hole-punched notebook-sized dictionary, thesaurus, world atlas, and optional English to Spanish or any other language that would be beneficial to the provider and the learner
* 3 hole-punched loose-leafed notebook paper for final drafts
* Sticky notes in a variety of sizes and colors, including 2" × 1.5"
* individual packaged sentence strips in a variety of colors
* roll of sentence strips
* small box of crayons with corresponding color names
* 12-inch ruler with metric side (holes in center for storage in binder)
* If you already have used materials at home, do use those before acquiring new ones.

Actual Creation and Organization of the Binder/Spiral

To begin, learners should write *their own names* and the title of the subject on the front of their own spirals and binders. (Permanent markers and *supervision* are required here for obvious reasons.)

The cover of the spiral is opened to the first page, which is attached on the left margin to the spiral. In the top right-hand corner of the side margin, the learner writes: 1. Then the page is turned to where the second page is attached to the spiral on the right margin. In the top right corner of that page, the learner writes: 2. Next, the page on the learner's right, which is attached to the spiral at the left margin, is numbered in the top right corner with the numeral 3. (These seemingly insignificant consistent directions TEACH *listening* and *following directions*.) This pattern is continued throughout the notebook. The numbers of the pages attached to the spiral on the left are "odd" numbers and the pages attached on the right are "even" numbers. The very last page of a 70-page spiral should have the number 140 in the top-right corner of the page that is attached to the spiral at the right margin. If that is not the case, and the learner is at a level where it is possible, this is a great time for the learner to practice numerical sequencing skills and go back and find where the error was made. Activities such as these help the learners to be more careful when they are working, and they also teach responsibility and independent ownership. Listening carefully to instructions and watching demonstrations all the way through are crucial to ongoing success. These are real world/real-time functions of reading and writing development.

Continuing with the spiral setup, return to page 1 and centered on the TOP line, write "Table of Contents." Skip a line and on the third line, *in* the *left* margin, write *page* #s. I realize that in today's tech world that # says hashtag. It also stands for "pounds" and "number," based on the context where it is found. Move to the *right* margin directly across the page, and on that same line 3, write "Date." In the CENTER of line 3, write "Title of Work" where the focus for each entry will actually be stated for the corresponding text entry in the spiral. By using spirals for learners who will be sharing the use of the learners' section or will themselves use it through different levels of development, no additions to that "book" will be distracting to other learning experiences.

On line 4, which is the next line, write "Table of Contents" again, in the center section, and move to the left margin. There I would reserve the remainder of page 1 through page 5, "1–5." On these pages, ONLY the focus titles, the page number for successive work entries, and the dates they begin will be recorded. It is imperative that this organization be maintained if this resource is to be effective. Skip line 5 and on line 6 write "Reserved for 'grade' level word lists" with the corresponding date in the right margin.

If it's helpful for the less experienced learner to write a small numeral on each line in the left margin to help them locate where they should make their entries in the table of contents, those numerals can be helpful for many math ventures. Not only are the early learners able to count forward as they write them, but they can also learn to count backward…a good experience for subtraction/division activities which gives them real-life experiences with numbers becoming smaller. You may be in situations where your learner is using the term "decompose" for some of the math processes they are doing. Those numerals make it less abstract for the learner to master skip counting by any number, i.e., 2, 4, 6; 3, 6, 9; 4, 8, 12; etc. By learning those skills, it will be much easier to learn addition, subtraction, multiplication, and division.

I have several activities for the learners to do in their spirals. The provider needs to estimate the number of pages to reserve for those activities. If the learner needs more pages for any of these tasks than have been estimated, do not tear out, etc. Just write at the bottom of the last page the number of the page where that particular activity will begin again. Then at the top of the beginning of the text, write, "continued from page." Be certain to record the previous information in the Table of Contents. The provider can also decide the order of the entries I suggest.

Responses to "Check for Understanding, Research Suggestions, and Activities" should be written in the spiral too. Double spacing of all entries in the spiral will make it neater and easier to read. The actual student responses to "ABCs," as well as any creative writing, will be much easier to edit and revise. Final drafts written on loose leaf can be whichever the learner and provider prefer. All loose leaf recordings must be kept in the binder and no pages in the spiral are to be used for any purpose not related to the "Teaching Reading Embedded books," **nor** should they be removed without the provider's permission/request. Those page numbers must then be recorded in the table of contents with the date and reason for their removal. These directions seem a bit stringent, but if they are not followed, the effort can become worthless.

Collective Nouns

Collective nouns are names for a collection of people or things. They are words for *single* units that are made up of *more* than *one* member. The size of the "group" can fluctuate greatly, even throughout a given day. A Memory of Elephants, for example, "can range in size from eight to one hundred, which is determined by several factors including the terrain where the elephants exist." Another factor that can determine the size of the "group" is the physical size of the individual members...the smaller the individual, the larger the "group" (a swarm of bees). Because of these and other factors, no attempt has been made to represent a "collection" of any animal.

A complete sentence using a collective noun phrase might read: The *litter* of kittens *sits* quietly. *Litter* is the subject of the sentence. *Kittens cannot* be the subject of the sentence because it is the object of the preposition, *of.* There will be some more information about eight parts of speech, later.

"Book Within a Book" is intended for the purpose of teaching reading to a variety of levels of readers. It is necessary to point out, from time to time, some of the grammar that is required for complete mastery of each of the levels of reading and communication.

Using the ABCs

Not all of you will have learners who meet the description of each of the levels that I discuss. I believe it would be beneficial to all providers to have an awareness and understanding of the interactions that I have outlined. You might see that your learner could benefit from an interaction that came at an earlier level.

Any activity from an *earlier level* could be beneficial, when interwoven, at least at the beginning of the *levels* which *follow*. I have structured each page in a similar fashion for continuity for the learner and the provider. I have not always included the same information about all of the animals, but the first two lines of each "animal page" have repetitive words that will develop awareness in the young learner over time. Repetition will lend to the learner's being able to *read* those words at the next levels. I will speak of using the learner's spiral and binder throughout this document and the "ABCs."

I have intentionally inserted the most basic sentence vocabulary throughout "ABCs" where the beginning reader can have success. This can help encourage the learner to focus on the print where it is necessary for the provider to read as they point to each word. The learner should be looking for words that they can successfully read and contribute to the ongoing conversation that the books provide. However, this focus should not be at the exclusion of the content message. It remains necessary for the provider and the learner to discuss the meaning of those printed words.

Addressing Levels of Learning Abilities

Levels (0) and (1) actually cover all the developmental levels up to awareness that print has meaning. As the learner develops a longer attention span and focuses more on the actual book, activities and expectations should become more complex. The following is the only place I will address interactions necessary to help your learner be better prepared for the levels that move through the "layers" of reading development.

I will *not* address these activities again for the (0) or (1) developmental level on each animal page entry either. Please realize that when I refer to learners' developmental level throughout my books that these are *just* the terms that I use in order to have a "point of reference" for the providers in as easy and simple way as I know. These levels are not "scientific."

Interactions Preceding Print Awareness

When I began to teach, everyone in the educational field—teachers, administrators, consultants, current educational writers and publishers, college professors, etc.—said that early grades were "learning to read" and older grades were "reading to learn." NO! ALL are doing both, or SHOULD be! Young learners are learning to recognize the print and tools that they need to recognize the textual features, but it IS FOR THE PURPOSE OF LEARNING what the MESSAGE IS that the author is conveying. Learners move on to more advanced types of reading and should be taught HOW to read the various texts and terminology that they encounter so that their comprehension of the MESSAGE is clearer!

(0) All of the activities and suggestions in this level are intended to begin to build a foundational development involving "interaction with the provider when printed material…pictures, letters, English-speaking book format, etc. are involved." Within the "ABCs" section, the *earliest* of learners can enjoy looking at the enlarged pictures and letters preceding the pages of text. The working memory, while interacting, and the short-term memory, which involves being able to do some basic responses to questions that the provider can pose, are planting more seeds for the emergence of print awareness. After exposure and discussion of some details, the provider might say, "Show me the (whatever the animal is)?" and the learner could point to the picture. Without a good working memory and short-term memory, the hope for success is limited. With proper interaction, that does not need to happen.

I have color-coded the letters in the top left corner of the text pages as well as the enlarged pictures and the captions under them. I have matched that color to a few of the Capital and lowercase letters in the text about the collective nouns and animals they describe. When you are focused on the *letter* of the alphabet, use *correct* terms of *Capital* and *lower case*. Even educators use big and little, sometimes. Any letters can be *big* and little! *Capital* and *lower case* have specific meanings in reading and writing. The fewer incorrect things we teach learners, the less confusion they will have going forward. Point to the letter as you say something like, "This is the *capital* letter A." It says /a/, as in apple. Trace around it. Repeat with the lowercase letter *a*, as you repeat the activity. Also, point out that the letters are in the *top left corner* of the page. Repeat this activity with all subsequent animal pages.

Point to the title as you tell the learner that this is the title of the story, and this is the "top center of the page." Then read the title. The depth of the activity you lead, or assist, your learner through in this section is determined by the level at which you have determined your unique learner *to* be. *Do* address all of the previous information, to some extent, regardless of how advanced that level might be.

For an immediate FYI, to determine an approximate level, where your learner *does* already recognize print, {(0) does *not* fit this category}, to the extent that they can read or decode *many* words, have your learner work through the entire first three or four pages of the "ABCs." If at all possible, have them attempt to do this independently or by following your minimal directions or questions. Where they demonstrate the most success and begin to require more instruction is the point where you begin. *Note*: you may find that they are not *yet* ready for any more than what I describe in (1), and that is fine! Remember the uniqueness of this book is that there is success for *all* levels of ability. You must read through the providers' section to determine where you and your learner begin.

Back to the *earliest* learner activities… Lead the focus to the drawing of the animal and name it. Make the sound, if possible, that the animal uses in its communication. Exaggerate the sound and have some *fun* with it. Encourage the learner to mimic the sound. Languages, even in their most primitive state, are made of sounds. Talk about animals with which the learner is familiar and how they communicate with each other. Talk about how pets communicate with their persons.

Point to the features of the animal and name them. Then point to those features on your own face, followed by naming the features on the learner's face. Encourage the learner to do the same.

Look for those animals in other print, in real life, on television, in science shows, in cartoons. Take trips to the park or the zoo and look for any of the animals. If you find them in captivity, such as the zoo, talk about where they really live in their natural habitats and why they are in the zoo. Refer back to the information in the book that was read. Take the book with you on your outings and ask the learner to find the animal in the book to match up with the real-life/real-time experiences. Talk about the illustrations being drawn with black "pencils" and the fact that many of the animals have very different colors. The accuracy of the drawings can be used to help your learner recognize the animals when they do see them in real life!

Talk about why the animals are important. Discuss with the learner if it's important to protect and preserve the animals. Discuss feelings and whether they realize that animals can feel pain and sadness. If you have a family pet, relate that the living animal they love is similar to other animals in the needs that they have.

Returning to "book" activities: For repetitive reinforcement, return the learner's focus to the alphabet letter, depending on the length of the learner's attention span. If the learner is finished with this page, turn to the next page or wait until another time to look at the letters again.

If they *are* still interested, it is good to say the letter name and sound as you trace around them again. When tracing the letters, demonstrate the appropriate, or at least a consistent, formation of the letters at the early stages. *Observe,* as your learner begins to independently trace them, whether there is any consistency. I have found, over the years, that there seems to be *some* evidence, when learners are beginning to read, even single letters or one-syllable words, that the formation of the letters' shapes is beneficial in the recognition of the letters at the independent visual level. When the learner finds them in meaningful print/word structure, *especially* when the learner is *struggling* with letter recognition, the realization that the printed word actually has stand-alone meaning is helpful. The recognition of the letter at the beginning of the learner's name, or the name of an object or pet, at the very least, is significant. The next level of print recognition would be to see that "*c-a-t*" is the letter pattern that names the picture of a cat. The *consistent* formation is merely from my extensive observations and, in *no way*, reflects any scientific research of which I am aware.

The provider can engage the learner by making up a *fun* story about the drawing of the animal. Encourage the early learner to repeat the provider's story, or make up their own, when possible. If you can replicate the movements of the animal in question and encourage the learner to emulate your movements, the learning experience will be well grounded for the learner and help develop further interest.

As interaction develops in *each* level, encourage the learner to be more self-disciplined in the physical use of a book. It is, also, never too early to passively point out the location of the various parts of the informational books, i.e., glossary, index, etc. All of this preparation will pay dividends throughout these experiences and in later years.

Allow the learner to turn the pages, at will or when encouraged by the provider. At this stage, the real focus is to "increase attention span," "introduce books in a happy and inviting atmosphere," "develop a receptive auditory vocabulary," and "show *your* own interest in books and reading." This early experience for the learner is a subtle way to encourage the lasting interest in books and the learning that can be derived from them. *Fun* interaction, with a book involved, can create so many lasting and positive benefits and memories. This alone can help learners to be more ready and actually find greater success at each subsequent level.

As I said earlier, I will not address this level of learning again. It is up to the provider to determine how many of the activities need more repetition and when to transition to the next levels. Make every effort to include, at *all* levels through which your learner(s) advance, a *fun* and enlightening experience.

Next Level but Still Limited Print Usage Capability

Level (1) will only be discussed here. The biggest difference between (0) and (1) is that the latter will have more realization that *print* has meaning. The depth to which you can take your discussions and the length and depth of the responses that you can expect from your learner are also major factors. Attention span should be longer. The provider's evidence of growth will be in those discussions and the active participation of the learner. It might be good to make some brief notes about your learner's progress in *your* own spiral with a label for each learner. It is *very* helpful to review progress.

(1) When reading the "story" about each animal, do not focus much attention on the collective noun and its meaning. Simply say the word and say something like, "That's a big word for a bunch of (whatever the animal is)." Some educators believe that words should not be used *before* the learner has reached the stage of meaningful understanding and use of the term. My observations and beliefs are that if the learner has never been given the opportunity to hear those "higher-level" words, the struggle to acquire them and their meanings will be more challenging at the time they do "fit into the need-to-know" stage. You are *not* quizzing the learner! You are merely using vocabulary that will lead to a natural yet highly advanced receptive language. Always be sure that you ARE using the word that is at their level, paired with the more advanced term. The use of the higher-level words will create the foundations to continue to add more {rich} vocabulary. To prevent or delay the learner from experiencing the higher levels of learning can actually prevent or delay them from reaching their own true potential!

Correct grammar usage by the provider and the significant others that the learner is with is the same as the discussion above, concerning "passive vocabulary acquisition." Learners follow their role models' examples, and they use the same types of communication skills that they see and hear on a daily basis. Try to always use correct grammar.

As you are working through the information in the stories, point out the color-coded letters. For example: green for *Aa*, blue for *Bb*, and orange for *Cc*. At this level, the learner should recognize that print has a deeper meaning than just letters on a page. Ask the learner to find various letters and to begin reading the *spelling* of familiar words, as in *frog* (f-r-o-g). This provides focus on *words* that are made up of *patterns* with specific letters to form specific words. Learners must have a sense of the relationship of the letters and their sounds in a particular sequence which makes up particular words. As early as possible, help the learner to understand that a specific "string of letters" makes a **specific** word, and a **specific** "string of words" makes a **specific** sentence which is a complete thought of **specific** meaning. In later years, some struggling learners still do not understand that concept. Without appropriate intervention at this point, learners can remain at what I refer to as "word callers," at best, and they struggle to make meaning of the words in their context.

Some words may have become familiar to your learner. Here, since repetition is being used while practicing saying the name of each letter at the top of the page along with its sound, the first letter of a word should become a commonly recognized pronunciation. With words such as *can* c/a/n, *and* a/n/d, *bug* b/u/g, etc., where each sound is consistent with those practiced, the learner may begin to *read* some words at an earlier level than might have been expected. Remember, learning is unique to the individual. Some will really excel as the doors are opened for them. Do not, however, allow learners who need more time to feel poorly toward themselves. Sometimes, the light just isn't as clear, and a bit more time is needed. I have actually witnessed cases where the slow starter surpasses the ones who seemed to be catching on more quickly.

Also, *do not* hold a learner at a level if they have demonstrated independent competence with all concerns at their current level. If they can answer the questions for that level, done "research" and *understood* the *meaning* associated with *their* level, *do* transition them to the next level.

You will probably find that you and your learner will be working in the transitional end of one level and the beginning of the following level. When you have an individualized or small group opportunity such as this, you will seldom find yourselves in just one level of instruction and mastery.

This paragraph is "thinking ahead." When an earlier-level achiever completes, possibly, the *literal* level where they understand the words and can match them in the text to the questions in "Check for Understanding," they can reread the story a second time with more independence and with more detailed understanding. They should also be able to respond to question number 3. If this procedure is showing progress, allow the learner to choose the order of the animal entries they would prefer to read for the next level of study. That can add an element of "freshness." Learners might even find it interesting to see the extent of their growth as they are able to achieve those higher levels of mastery using the same information. It is not necessary that every animal be revisited multiple times. The activities and questions can be used in books of your own choosing once the provider is certain that their learner has achieved the goal of the higher-level interpretation at each learning level.

The ability of the learner to predict future happenings is an important comprehension strategy to be used not only in reading but also in general life events. That strategy should be strengthened at this level. Guiding the learner to begin to predict, when the learner has had an opportunity to "see the letters and the animals and learn the repetitive features of each page," is a good introduction to this focus.

Using Print in Meaningful Recognition

I suggest, based on a number of experiences, that a professional eye exam beyond the traditional "school exam" be done before beginning this level. Generalized screening nor daily observations recognize all the possible visual needs which can cause issues if not addressed properly and in a timely manner.

Active involvement at this level should find questions focusing the learner to look for words that they can recognize and read. The provider should start a list in the learner's spiral. As the learner's ability to copy letters develops, encourage them to write their own words.

From this point forward, there will be suggested questions and activities at the bottom of each page in the animal section. The questions numbered 2 through 4+ will be suggestive of the levels of reading readiness to move to the next level.

(2) This level is for those who are ready to move on to more print involved efforts. Remember that a goal is to CREATE as much independence in the learner as possible. Teaching of sight words, such as *the*, *that*, and other words where the individual sounds are not clearly heard, are good to do ahead of the actual reading, or read them for the learner a few times when they appear.

The first two sentences have several of the same words. This is so the learner, who is beginning to read, begins to recognize the repetitive words without effort, not only on the pages within this book but also anywhere they might find them in their environment. Examples: The animal called _____ is a/an _____. _____ typically live in… At this level, always point to the repetitive words so that the learner begins to look for them. Gradually allow the learner to read, or at least make the attempt to read, them independently. If there is difficulty, have the learner say each letter in order as it appears in the word. Encourage the learner to say each sound in its sequential order, if necessary, in order to correctly recognize the word. If, for some reason, there is still insufficient success, this could be a more complicated need and solution for the learner. These issues can be overlooked or undetected by a provider. Even those who are teachers may lack some of the training or experience to realize the repercussions and their need to be addressed early. Some other words which should become committed to memory are the words that I have chosen as the repetitive words in the first two sentences and in the sentences with the more basic vocabulary. As you progress through the book, encourage the learner to read the words that they have come to recognize. Just as it is extremely important to develop extensive auditory language, it is equally important, by now, to develop the visual receptive language. I have referred to receptive vocabulary where the learner is "receiving" everything from their environmental experiences.

Now I will add the *expressive* verbal and written vocabulary, which should be developing, naturally, through the discussions the provider offers. *Always* encourage the learner to speak their own expressions at whatever their level is. Again, more will be addressed in future books.

Literal Meaning

(3) At this point, the learner should be able to recognize most of the basic words. Many words should be those that can be sounded out. (Future books will have more extensive guidance in this process.) If a word seems to be too challenging, simply pronounce it a time or two when it is encountered but, then, encourage the learner to recognize the "configuration"/ shape of the word. Oftentimes, the longer words are more readily recalled because there is a more impressive pattern that "sticks" in the learner's visual memory. The anchor that I developed when I was working with those who had difficulty in these areas was the analogy of a two-story house with a basement. If the word was *everything*, *ever* and *in* are the main level letter formations, *th* is the second story, and *y* and *g* are the basement letters. Then I would draw boxes around the letters showing the learner that pattern in the actual word, *everything*, which anchored a mental image. This is also a good strategy for spelling practice. *Always* discuss what is happening and being learned in the book, at every level, so that the learner is very aware that the ultimate goal is *making meaning*.

Higher-Level Comprehension Skills

(4) Learners at this level should be able to read the words with fluency and be past the need to sound out the majority of words they encounter. When learners reach this level, it is good to practice reading the same paragraphs for increasing speed of reading. As this is introduced, there may be some reduced accuracy in word recognition, and that is even to be expected to some degree. However, the accuracy should return, and speed can continue to increase. Remember, learning is an individual thing, and not all learners will progress, in any aspect of reading, at the same exact rate, nor will all learners arrive at the "exact optimal level." However, they should have the opportunity to achieve their "own unique optimal level"! Always exercise patience and positive reinforcement at *all* levels of effort. Each beginner, of each level, should have some challenge for which to reach, but the greater level of success will be achieved from a *very solid* foundation.

Comprehension of the information should be strong but may still lack the ability to understand outcomes and consequences of certain situations. They may still need more background knowledge gained from more extensive experiences and interactions.

Using Knowledge of Print and Higher-Level Thinking Skills to Interpret Meaning in the Learner's Greater Surroundings

(4+) The level of learners who can read and comprehend the "ABCs" in the literal sense needs to be encouraged to think about the meaning beyond the printed words.

Below are examples of ways to do this.

In "Army of Frogs", you might ask: Why do you think frogs need to live where there are a lot of trees rather than in a desert? {Shade from trees would help protect the frogs' skin from drying out}.

For those who master that level of reasoning, ask: What might happen to the frog population if the water where tadpoles live becomes heavily polluted and a thick scum forms on the surface of the water? {The tadpoles would not be able to breathe, and they would die. If they die, there would be no frogs developing!}

Following that level of reasoning, ask: What will happen to the ecosystem if the frog population is greatly reduced? {The prey on which frogs feed will flourish and become over populated.}

What will happen to the food source (plants) if the insects flourish and overpopulate? The questions can become endless once the learner has gone beyond the literal stage of comprehension. Their answers, however, will be dependent on the extensiveness of their background of experiences.

Evaluating Information

This level will rely heavily on those "*thinking* skills the learner has experienced throughout the 'Collective Nouns' animal pages."

The highest levels of thinking skills that I will address in my books are through question suggestions for the purpose of evaluation of the material in a given passage. *This* process will weigh heavily on the learner's own value system combined with *all* information they have on the subject. To be able to do this, research involving a number of sources, both pro (agreeing) *and* con (disagreeing), is necessary. The learner should then be in a position to make an informed decision based on fact, not emotion, or someone else's *opinion,* or what seems to be the "popular at the time" belief. At this point, the provider needs to show interest in the *learner's* interests and actively help the learner acquire those resources. This is also an excellent time to include school-related materials, both for topics to research *and* asking the higher-level questions (4+).

At the end of most pages are three questions that are numbered *2, 3,* and *4+.* They are numbered this way because, as I pointed out in the beginning of the providers' section of the *Embedded Book,* number 1 is not repeated because the "assessment" for the learner should be revealed through the ongoing discussions the provider and learner have in sections (0) and (1). (1) is a number because the learner should be actually capable of using some of the print, whereas (0) is not. Each question has a different level of understanding for the learner to demonstrate.

The first question, which is actually numbered *2* for the reasons I explained at the beginning of the providers' section is literal and requires only that the learner can match up words in the question with words in the text. For some, this may be a difficult activity.

Question 3 requires that the learner use new information from the text to combine with previous knowledge to interpret the meaning of the text. For those who have had less interactive discussions, or have had limited access to some of the experiences that create a rich background of knowledge and vocabulary for the learner, this will be a challenging effort. Care must be given to provide opportunities for the learner to develop a stronger and more diverse knowledge of their surroundings.

Question 4+ requires a level of understanding that will allow the learner to make a prediction based on the information *and* their background knowledge. Again, the learner will be confined by limited previous conversations and interactive exposure to a broad array of activities.

Further thinking at the level of (4+) also requires the learner to form an opinion based on their evaluation of the information. During the early stages of this development, it is imperative that care be given to encourage the learner to "take the chance to express themselves" without fear of disappointing the provider.

Further Development of Questioning

The previous and following sets of questions should be helpful to the provider in understanding how to develop their own questions. The earlier set of question-related thoughts takes the provider through the levels of thinking from literal through evaluation where the learners should function. As I pointed out, even the youngest can be stimulated in all of these thought processes, if the activities and discussions include necessary information to create the questions that are posed correctly. These kinds of experiences *need* to be tapped, from the beginning, *if* the learners are to achieve their unique potential.

I have found too often that learners are NOT challenged with questions that require critical thinking. There is no reason why the higher-level reasoning cannot be used. The provider must formulate the questions to help the learner arrive at those answers through the discussions they instigate in daily interactions. *Again*, make these discussions and interactions *fun* and *natural! Do not* just set your learners down and "push" information at them.

Formal Question/Response

The following questions provide opportunity for the reader to apply a popular educational set of strategies for understanding print known as QAR (Question/Answer/Relationship). This is repetitious, using different terminologies, but actually getting to the same point as the previous questions. The earlier ones are conversational questions that I formulated. The following questions are a more formal set of questioning:

1. Right there: The answer is in the print which corresponds with #2 in Check for Understanding in the ABCs.
2. Think and search: recall and find information to confirm…

3. Author and reader: The new information is combined with what the reader already knew in order to provide the answer. #2 and #3 relate to #3 in the Check for Understanding.

4. On my own or "in my head": Only the reader has personal knowledge or personal experience to provide an answer to the question, i.e., How did you feel or know…when something happened… #4 is #4+ in Check for Understanding.

Possible "Mixed Signals" from Learners

A word of caution here is necessary. Some of you will encounter situations where, for whatever reason, the print will be extremely difficult, and yet, the learner's higher-level thinking skills and auditory/verbal receptive and expressive/"speaking" language can go far beyond the learner's expected learning level based on the previous responses to print. Background *cannot* be overstated. I have had learners at all grade levels who left me speechless with their astounding depth of knowledge and understanding of the meaning of the text when they participated in discussions. *Never* set your sights too *low* for your learner! Remember, the key is the amount of interaction given and expectation placed on the learner.

I have, however, found opposite situations where effort to increase the learners' background and vocabulary had to be strengthened. Fluent reading of the text was demonstrated, but when asked any questions about what they had read, no answers of significance were offered.

When Learners Have Become Successful Readers

Encourage the learner to seek advanced reference material on some related topic, or to learn about their own specific interests. Here, the provider should offer interest in what the learner is researching. When securing materials for the research, the provider can make that possible. If the learner is new at note-taking, and the provider can teach them, use those strategies. If not, let the learner copy some of the sentences at first. This should not be done for any formal reports that the learner needs to "hand in," or is to be used for public documentation unless the source is cited.

School-related and required materials can be the focus here.

Background information to simplify further learner experiences

Whether the "door" is a thin veil or a ton of steel with rusty hinges to be opened for the success of your learners, *all* deserve to have the experience of success and praise with honest feedback as they take this journey. It is the *realistic* self-concept that individuals *perceive*, which continues to move each person forward. Without it, especially in the early stages of development, the possibility of a "shutdown" in the efforts to master the strongest communication skills exists. Often, when this occurs, learners have a need to find other ways to self-express. *If* that *shutdown* does occur, the task of working together to develop the reading (and writing) skills will be much more difficult.

During a time when one of my students seemed to have arrived at the "shutdown" stage, I was reminded of when I was a little girl on the farm. We pumped, by hand, the water we carried from the well for use in the house and all other places needed. Sometimes, Dad had to prime the pump (pour a little water down from the top while someone quickly, "WITHOUT jerking the handle!" pumped), and soon the water would come streaming out of the spout. I thought about a pump in terms of students' vocabulary development that was not producing, so "I primed the *pump*." At times, you need to *look* for positives to praise and encourage so that your "pump" can find, deep within, the desire to produce…*honest* praise can yield wonders in "priming the pump"!

Setting the Stage for the "ABCs" Experience

Before you begin the "ABCs," be certain that the learner understands the following information:

- EVERYTHING on earth is *animal*/meat, *vegetable*/plant, or *mineral*/all other things (rocks, etc.)
- *Herbivores* eat plants. *Carnivores* eat meat. *Omnivores* eat both plants and meat. And *insectivores* eat insects.

Most animals are *diurnal*, awake in the daytime; *nocturnal*, awake at night; or *crepuscular*, awake just before dawn and just after dusk.

Awareness of these words and their meanings will help reduce some confusion created by [lean] vocabulary, placed intentionally for instructional purposes, within the "ABCs" text.

[Lean] {Rich} Context Clues

[Lean] vocabulary: These are words that have few or no "hints" in context. Some words will be a natural part of the learner's prior "hearing" (auditory) vocabulary, and depending on the level of the learners that the providers are addressing, they may be a part of their "seeing" (visual) vocabulary. Just because they may recognize the term does *not necessarily* mean that they know the meaning. It would be good to talk about some of those words. The learners need to become aware of how very important it is that *they* are alert to their everyday experiences and conversations. They must realize that they can control the extensiveness of their background knowledge by knowing/learning the vocabulary involved in their everyday situations rather than letting those opportunities pass them by.

Vocabulary is the *single greatest* indicator of the highest level of potential achievement in life. *Every single* thing about our lives concerns VOCABULARY, whether it is letters and words, numbers, sign language, brail, pictures, or nature—*every single* thing! If the learner has a "lean" vocabulary, the more challenging (*not impossible*), but *challenging*, the task of bringing success will be. It will take longer, and more insights will be required on the part of the provider, with this educational venture. I have personally found that this issue crosses all socioeconomic, cultural, etc., aspects of *who* an individual is and *can become*.

When I found a student who could not use context clues for decoding, nor for comprehension, I looked to their background vocabulary. If that is an issue with your learner, you need to find all appropriate experiences that will help create a much {richer} vocabulary. Those experiences begin with conversations in which you engage them. I have told a few stories throughout these writings. The intent was to reinforce a point I was making *or* to provide my audience a small point of reference to recall a few informational details. When you, the provider, share some of your own stories, you will not only provide some well-chosen references but you will also enhance your *very special* relationships.

Natural Ways to Decrease the Potential Impact of [Lean] Text

If the provider has access to the learner throughout regular lifetime experiences, again *talk* to the person, in a natural way for the most part, about the common things in their environment… take a walk around your living area; your yard; your neighborhood; parks; museums; zoos; *any* and *all* healthy, *fun* environments that you can provide. If some of those tasks are impossible, take the learner to the library. "Find" the experiences lacking in the learner's natural "world" in books of all types; use maps and globes…tangible, basic, hands-on opportunities. The more ways—*seeing, hearing, touching, moving, smelling, tasting,* feeling through *emotional sensitivity* (cheerful, sad, thoughtful, sympathetic, empathetic, *fun*!), etc.—to which a learner can have exposure, the more the learner will master in this critical foundation-building part of the learner's future efforts. That foundation will be more quickly internalized! "Planting the seeds…" through the personal interactions you create, will help your learner to reap boundless rewards that will multiply with time.

The provider will, depending on the level of the learner, need to offer appropriate information, from simply telling the meaning of the word to looking it up in a good old-fashioned dictionary, or thesaurus, *or* encyclopedia, *with* the learner. The uses of these resources are other teaching events for the provider and their learner. All of this will help to decrease the [lean] text and increase the {rich} text for your learner. These activities will also give the learner the tools to lead them to more independent control over future learning experiences.

If, when actually reading with the learner, the provider's goal for the session is for the learner to understand content, then simply say the unknown word and its meaning and continue on. When it is a teaching session involving the how-tos to further the independence of the learner, then take the time to do whatever is appropriate for the learner to advance.

If the text is {rich}, the focus word will precede, or follow, a synonym. It may also be surrounded by more common words which will lead the learner to recognize the word, in print, and to understand the message. Even if she/he cannot give a generalized meaning of the word itself, the content will be mastered. The word may be new to the learner only *in* print. Remember, you are not looking for a formal dictionary definition. Very few of us could provide those for every word in our extensive receptive and expressive vocabularies!

If it is a {rich} context word and the learner *does not* recognize the clues that are given, point out the synonym of the word, or the surrounding words, and ask them to explain the meaning of those words. Sometimes, a learner has had too little meaningful verbal interaction for them to create the necessary background information for the most success. Go through as many examples of the surrounding text which may be right next to the new word, or you may need to search previous sentences or following sentences to gain those {rich} clues.

A few of the words are marked [ ] and { } throughout some of the animal stories in the "ABCs." Any support techniques I have provided in the first half of the book, for emerging readers, will be phased out in the last half of the book. The learners are expected to practice those types of examples in other text, if necessary, so that they can progress through the latter half. The first half of the book should be used by the advanced learner for the probability of gaining new information. Questions and research activities may be a new way for those individuals to "see things" as well.

For the more advanced learner, have them locate other words on the pages based on their own unique knowledge that are {rich} and [lean]. Encourage them to decide what words could have been used with the [lean] words to make the passages better. They could also look at the {rich} text and find synonyms and antonyms for those words, thereby increasing their own vocabulary. Synonyms and antonyms can be tricky. Even when they are definitely similar, or opposite in meaning, all of them are not always interchangeable in context. Oftentimes, just reading the entire sentence or paragraph will help determine the appropriateness. If not, look for exact definitions in the notebook dictionary.

The following are a few examples from the "ABCs":

"Army of Frogs":
[Lean]: amphibian; freshwater; forested; centipedes; declining
>   Compound words, when taken apart, can quickly change them from [lean] to {rich}.

{Rich}: (for the advanced)…species; carnivores; natural habitat

"Business of Ferrets":
[Lean]: weasels; badgers
>   They may recognize that they are animals but know nothing about how they look or behave.

{Rich}: carnivores; domesticated

The following lists are "rule of thumb" grade level attainment for the purpose of giving novice providers a glimpse of the complexity of words at which a learner should be visually capable of mastering. Some word placements are based on the number of times a learner encounters them in text even though they seem more complex than some of the words in later levels. When learners are capable of copying most of the words, be sure that they leave adequate space between words so that they can be easily read. A follow-up activity with this list would be to have an appropriately accomplished learner place these words in alphabetical order by *LEVEL*. A higher-level capability could combine and alphabetize all words in this original list.

Actual List to be Copied by the Learner

Preschool

and, big, ball, fast, go, green, cat, dog, help, mother, little, play, ride, red, not, said, stop, the, to, work, no, it, can, we

Kindergarten

are, came, black, game, bed, did, eat, farm, house, now, on, like, put, paint, ready, store, tree, your, too, white, green, yes, sit

First Grade

boy, bell, after, blue, dinner, call, faster, ball, top, pot, funny, guess, into, here, like, money, sat, stay, toy, now, pocket

Second Grade

across, ask, does, five, ever, bird, city, shoe, wet, uncle, set, ship, step, over, pull, next, rolled, listen, miss, happy, girl, just

Activities to Do with Word Lists

Learners could make word search pages by placing the words in a graph paper grid. The letters from the words used would be placed in horizontal, diagonal, and vertical spellings. When the word letters are complete, fill in the rest of the grid with random letters to fill the spaces. If these are being made for earlier learners, CAPITAL letters should be used in the focus words to help with visual awareness. Write a word bank with those words and use capital letters there as well.

Crossword puzzles can also be created with clues from the ABCs. Open boxes of the numbers to fit words from word banks can be any direction and "extra" boxes should have X in each.

Basic Syllable Patterns

CONSONANT/VOWEL (CV): The vowel will have a long vowel sound and is also referred to as an OPEN syllable: go, no, he, hi, fa, gnu. Not all words follow these patterns so I hesitate to call them "Rules." (**Do** is one example.) That is true of all Pattern Guidelines.

VOWEL/CONSONANT (VC): The vowel will have a "short" sound, and these patterns are called CLOSED syllables because the vowel is followed by one or more consonants in that syllable. It makes no difference about any letters that may come before the vowel in that syllable. (at, in, et, on, un); word not belonging: *of*. Not all syllables will be standalone words, but they are often referred to as nonsense words. It is important that learners know that they follow the same guidelines as other syllables in the respective patterns so that they can pronounce multisyllable words as their vocabulary grows.

CONSONANT/VOWEL/CONSONANT (CVC): The vowel will have the short sound because regardless of the letters that come BEFORE the vowel, the vowel is FOLLOWED by at least one consonant which makes it a closed syllable. (top, shack, lit, tup, brings, bet); not belonging: *front*.

Eight parts of speech with usage in an example sentence:
The most widely used eight parts of speech include the following:

Noun:	n	person, place, or thing
Verb:	v	shows action or state of being
Adjective:	adj	tells more about the noun
Adverb:	adv	tells more about the verb

Conjunction:	conj	joins words or sentences
Interjection:	int	sets the mood or tone of the sentence
Pronoun:	pron	takes the place of a noun
Preposition:	prep	connects or relates words used within the sentence

int   *n*   *conj*   *pron*   *v*   *prep*   *adj*   *n*   *conj*   *pron*   *v*   *adj*   *adj*   *n*
Wow, Hannah and   I   went   to   the zoo, and   we   saw   a   giant   shark

adv   *v*   *prep*   *adj*   *n*
quickly moving   in   the aquarium!

Words directly above the corresponding words in the sentence example tell the parts of speech that the words in the sentence represent. Actually, *a*, *an*, and *the* are called noun markers, but they also function as adjectives.

Much more information will be offered in future books about the parts of speech and their usage in improving written communication. All other topics found in these books will be addressed in greater depth. More instruction will be given concerning reading of different print genre, as well.

31

Our Educational System
Flipped Upside Down

ABC's:

A Collection of Collective Nouns

Written for Learners of All Ages and Levels

Author: Barbara Stotts Cochran

Illustrator: Debra Cochran Talich

About the Illustrator

I internalized the desire to do "my best" at a very young age. When I learned to write, I wanted my letters to be "perfect." That desire spread to anything and everything else I attempted. Because of my perfectionism, teachers gave me the time to finish my "masterpieces." With this time allowed, I would often stay in from recess to make my assignments perfect. Mom would tell me to "just slop it up and get it handed in…it would still be very easy to read." *I could not* imagine handing in a "sloppy job"!

After winning the handwriting award many weeks in a row, and many times throughout my first-grade year, I didn't realize, with my extra efforts with penmanship skill, that I was actually falling behind in reading. In the second grade, I found myself in the second reading group. I will never forget getting up the courage to go up to the teacher and ask her if I could be moved up in reading.

She replied very quickly, and nicely, "*No*, now sit back down."

I completed my fourth-grade year through which we enjoyed small-group reading instruction, which was done in a separate room, by a different teacher than my wonderful homeroom teacher, Mrs. Veda Flint. She was very encouraging and taught me social studies, science, and math. I will never forget her creative and very fun in-room tree house. Because Mrs. Flint was the accomplished expert, my capability was never in question by my mom who was Mrs. Flint's student teacher while she was finishing her bachelor's degree with an emphasis in reading. I remember I loved being in third grade knowing my mom was just across the "pod," teaching in Mrs. Flint's fourth-grade classroom. My fourth-grade reading teacher always gave me the highest grades and never mentioned to my parents that I was in a "lower group." That explained why I was a full year behind in the number of books I should have completed at the end of fourth grade. When Mom asked me how badly I wanted to be "on level," I told her I didn't think it was possible because I had already tried to get moved up in second grade and was told No. Mom understood what had occurred and saw how badly I wanted to have all the skills to be on level to begin fifth grade because, at that time, small reading groups were no longer used and the whole class was taught together. She told me there was no reason I shouldn't be on level and that she would tutor me over the summer. She told me that it would be a lot of work, and I was fine with that! I had a friend whose mother asked if she could join the tutoring sessions.

Mom secured the books and materials from the school, and Mrs. Flint agreed to give me the unit tests so that there would be no concerns about the accuracy of my achievements. It soon became obvious that my needs were not academic, but my "need to have the prettiest papers I could create" was getting in my way. I completed the books that would normally have taken a full year in the regular classroom in *one month* while still getting to enjoy my summer! My friend also successfully accomplished her goal of "on level." I went to fifth grade in the fall where we were all tested again. I tested at the *seventh*-grade level. Thanks to my mom's extra time and efforts teaching me that summer, I was not told no but instead was actually placed in the "accelerated group."

I began to realize that *perfection* during the journey was NOT as important as the timely and accurate completion of the task! I was *getting in my own way*, so to speak, and I still struggle with that to this day. I share this with those of you who are using this book to help anyone in need of the skills and strategies and the way my mom teaches reading through reading. Please help everyone who is "getting in his or her *own way*" to realize that we all must step aside, at times, to *get out* of our own way to take those first steps to see the growth we will realize. This can be even more important when we may *doubt* our own potential.

My very recent example of this is when my mom asked me to draw the illustrations which I have created for this book. I had initially declined the project, telling her, "Oh, I can't do that. I haven't even tried to draw for over twenty-five years; I can't draw now!"

As she always does, she continued to encourage me to try. She knew I was in need of tapping into my creativity as I was becoming more and more stressed working in health care throughout the pandemic. It is evident from the first drawing I did of the elephant where I used my single #2 lead pencil to my final drawing of the butterfly where I actually used an art pencil set. The growth that will occur, given practice and when using the most efficient "tools available to succeed," will become obvious. I am still growing and venturing into using new mediums for the illustrations that I am creating for my mom's next book. Our next book will have some of the animals depicted in watercolor! I know my first will not meet my own self-demanding perfectionism, nor probably will my last. I will, however, *not* get in my own way of accomplishing, to the best of my ability at the time, the drawings that will be published!

I hope you use this amazing *tool* my mom has now created for all of you by writing this book to enhance your skills or overcome any obstacles that you may have encountered with growing your reading skills throughout this pandemic and in the future. Remember to use your talents and strive to learn new skills and techniques so you can accomplish whatever it is you want to explore tomorrow and throughout your lifetime.

Best wishes in your journeys and don't forget to always try your best, but more importantly, get out of your own way when necessary!

I dedicate my drawings in this book to my amazing mom, My teacher, and Your teacher, Barbara Stotts Cochran. Without her persistent encouragement and instruction, I am sure I would not have achieved my first bachelor's degree with areas of emphasis in psychology, gerontology, and interior design and another bachelor of science degree, with honors, in occupational therapy.

I also want to dedicate my academic accomplishments as well as my artistic talents and accomplishments as a published illustrator in memory of my amazing father, the late Malcolm L Cochran. He greatly influenced my journey! (Dad, you are loved and missed daily!).

I also need to thank my fantastic husband, Rick, and our three cherished sons, Turner, Cooper, and Sawyer, for encouraging me throughout my new journey of drawing. Without all of their support, I would not have found the courage to realize the artistic potential that I do enjoy.

Debra Cochran Talich

Contents

Collective Noun	Animal
Army	Frogs
Business	Ferrets
Colony	Seals
Doylt	Swine
Family	Beavers
Group	Guinea Pigs
Horde	Hamsters
Implausibility	Gnus
Journey	Giraffes
Kaleidoscope	Butterflies
Lamentation	Swans
Memory	Elephants
Nide	Pheasants
Obstinacy	Buffalo
Prickle	Porcupines
Quarrel	Sparrows
Rangale	Deer
Study	Owls
Troop	Kangaroo
Unkindness	Ravens
Venue	Vultures
Waddle	Penguins
X	Learner's own creation
Yap	Chihuahuas
Zeal	Zebra

A a

Army of Frogs

A a

Army of Frogs

The animal called "frog" is an amphibian /am-phib-i-an/. Most frogs live in [forested] areas and [freshwater] wetlands. Frogs are found in {natural habitats}, or surroundings, on six of the seven continents of the earth. Frogs do not live on the continent of Antarctica.

Most frogs are {carnivores}. Their food is insects, worms, spiders, and [centipedes]. Larger frogs can eat mice and small snakes. A few species are [herbivores].

Frogs are said to have two lives, which is the meaning of the word, {amphibian}. Frogs begin life in a totally different form when they hatch from eggs which are laid in water by the female frog. This first phase of their lives is called *tadpole*, and they have tails. They breathe through gills and by sucking air bubbles from the surface of the fresh water in which they live. As they mature, they begin to develop their back legs, and then their front legs begin to appear. Next, they slowly {absorb} the material that makes up the tail. The tail shrinks. The material is used as a food source during the change from tadpole to the second phase of life, which is the frog. The frog lives most of its time on land in wet areas so that the skin remains moist. Adult frogs breathe air through their lungs, and oxygen also passes through their moist skin. Too much sun can damage frogs' skin which is the main reason over half of all frog species are in danger of extinction.

Frogs are the largest group of amphibians. There are more than six thousand recorded [species] of frogs. The "warty-frog" species tends to be called *toads*. Some species are [declining] in number due to a variety of reasons. Because of the frogs' diet, they are a very important part of the food chain. The population of animals that makes up their natural prey increases in numbers rapidly, and without a thriving frog population, the number of insects, etc., would increase dramatically.

Check for Understanding

2. What are some of the things frogs eat? Find some of those words in the print.
3. What would happen if the frog population were to really decrease in and around their ponds?
4+. What could happen to the earth's environment without a significant population of frogs?

Research Suggestions

- How does the Alaskan wood frog survive in the Arctic Region?
- How might climate change affect all frog populations?

Activities

- Find a picture of a wood frog and draw it in your spiral.
- Write a paragraph about it.

B b

Business of Ferrets

B b

Business of Ferrets

The animal called "ferret" is a mammal. Most ferrets live in forests, plains, deserts, [tundra], grasslands, and mountainous regions. Wild ferrets that live in North America are the black-footed ferret.

It is the only ferret {native} to, or that has always lived, in North America. It is endangered because of the very small populations which are cut off from other "businesses."

Ferrets are {carnivores} so they eat meat. Their main food source is the white-tailed prairie dog. Ferrets also use the tunnels made by those prairie dogs, for shelter. Some of the animals to which ferrets are related are [weasels] and [badgers].

Male ferrets are called ***hobs***, and female ferrets are called ***jills***. Baby ferrets younger than one year of age, are called ***kits***. Ferrets survive in the wild for about two years, but in captivity they can live up to seven years.

The close cousin of the wild North American black-footed ferret is the European ferret. European ferrets have been {domesticated}, raised by people, for over 2,500 years. European ferrets were brought to the British American colonies in the 1600s to kill rodents, their natural prey. Domesticated ferrets cannot find their own food, and they would soon die if humans did not take good care of them.

The author's personal experience with ferrets, named Tigger and Templeton, was when I held them. They belonged to my son and daughter-in-law. They were fun and entertaining. They loved gentle attention. Taking care of pet ferrets is a lot of responsibility, so {acquiring} one as a pet should be taken very seriously. If you plan to explore that opportunity, do your research first!

Check for Understanding

2. What is the main food source of the wild North American ferrets? Find the words that tell you that.
3. What could have happened to the early colonists if the European ferret had not been brought to the British American colonies?

4+. What could happen to the habitat of the North American black-footed ferret if humans do not find a way to prevent them from becoming extinct?

Research Suggestions

- How long has the black-footed ferret lived in North America?
- Where do they mainly live now?
- Were the black-footed ferrets ever considered endangered?
- If so, what was done to repopulate them?

Activities

- Reread the above text to recall why the "cousin" ferret was brought to the British American colonies.
- Draw a picture of what the colonies would have looked like in those times. Include the ferret where it might have been found.
- Write a few sentences to explain your drawing to your readers.

C c

Colony of Seals

C c

Colony of Seals

The animal called "seal" is a marine mammal. Seals belong to a group of animals called [pinniped].

Most seals live in many different areas of the oceans. However, two subspecies of the ringed seals live in

fresh water all the time. Harbor seals, also called common seals, will go into the mouths of rivers that

empty into salt waters. These waters are called estuaries. Estuaries are where the seals catch their prey.

The "shoes" that humans wear when they swim in deep water look somewhat like the seals' feet which are also called flippers. The seals' flippers help them swim. Seals cannot "walk" on land. They scoot on their bellies to get around on land when they are not swimming in the water. They also have no ear covering to make the ears more visible.

Seals are carnivores. They eat fish and [zooplankton]. They can find their prey by using their very sensitive whiskers. Since the water where they swim is not clear for easy visual location of the prey, they use those whiskers to very easily feel any kind of movement. Seals are also one of several marine mammals that are protected, by law, in the United States.

Check for Understanding

2. What do people wear when they swim in deep water that look like the seals' "feet"? Locate those words in the text above.
3. Do you think that people copied the seals' feet when deepwater swimmers wanted a better way to move around in deep water? Explain your answer.
4+. Why do you think seals are protected by laws in the United States?

Research Suggestions

- What are pinnipeds? What other animals are in that grouping?
- What are the natural predators of seals?

D d

Doylt of Swine

D d

Doylt of Swine

The animals called "swine", in the United States, are younger pigs which typically weigh about 180 pounds. They are not yet ready for market. Most swine live on farms in many habitats. It is thought that they were brought to North America about 1500. Many people believe that swine were among the earliest animals to be domesticated. It is estimated that that was about forty thousand years ago! Antarctica is the only continent where swine do not live.

Unlike most mammals with hoofs, swine do not have a stomach that lets them have a "cud." You will learn more about that as you read about more of the hoofed animals in this book. Because they need to eat more than just leaves and grass, they will eat just about anything unless their diet is controlled by their owners. Also, unlike most other hoofed mammals, swine build nests for their young. My brother, Jack, shared stories with me about the doylts that our dad raised and how the sows rooted the loose hay into nests before the piglets were born. The nests are commonly built within twenty-four hours of the ***piglets'*** birth.

A ***sow***, as the mother is called, can have as many as two litters, or groups of piglets, in a year. Each doylt can be as many as thirteen piglets. Piglets begin feeding within one hour of birth. They are usually weaned from their mother's milk between two and three weeks of age.

Swine are usually very clean animals. Their sweat glands are {inefficient} to cool their body temperature as other animals do. They need to "wallow" in mud. That is, perhaps, one of the reasons some people think they are unclean. Swine are actually smarter than dogs. They can be trained to learn their own names in a short period of time. They also have excellent memories.

Author's personal note: On my parents' farm where my dad had several big doylts of tame pigs, there would sometimes be a {runt} born. Since it was so little, it would usually be crowded out by its littermates when it came time to eat. My dad taught me how to care for the runts. I was then given the responsibility of making sure they were safe, warm, and well fed. When the runts were big enough, they were put back with the rest of their family. I learned the importance of responsibly caring for another life of any kind.

Swine usually made the "grunt" sound when **they** "talked" to my dad as he scratched behind their ears and called them by their names, as **he** "talked" to them. I noticed that he changed the tone of his voice, very much like it changed when he talked with me. Sometimes I wonder if swine respond more to tone of voice than they do to words. Besides grunting, I also know from personal experience that they squeal *loudly* when they are *not* happy! They also say *oink* when they are just communicating.

Some schools take their students on field trips to farms where they can see swine. Zoos all around the world have a variety of species where people can see them in places designed to be like their normal habitat.

Check for Understanding

2. What was my dad doing when his pig would grunt to him? Give at least one answer.
3. In paragraph 6, find one sentence that has no factual information about swine? In your answer, explain why the other sentences are factual.
4+. How can an excellent memory and being so smart benefit a pig?

Research Suggestions

- What other foods can supply the nutrients humans get from eating pork?
- What are some good recipes that are made with substitutions for that meat?
- Do animals respond to tone of voice more than they do to the actual words that are used? Whether you can find formal research that discusses this issue or not, make your own observations. Begin with your own immediate persons with whom you interact. To which do YOU respond most successfully?

E e

Embarrassment of Pandas

E e

Embarrassment of Pandas

The animal called "giant panda" is a bear-like mammal. Black-and-white pandas typically /tip-i-kal-li/ live in bamboo forests high in the mountains of South Central China. They were forced from their earlier lowland habitat because of farming and [deforestation]. There are heavy clouds and much rain in their current surroundings. The climate is not very hot, nor is it very cold. Bamboo grows well in this area, and it is the main food of the giant panda.

At the time of this writing, giant pandas are no longer on the endangered animal list. However, as of the 2020 count, there are only 1,864 pandas left living in the wild. There is still some worry about the habitat being able to support the lives of these special animals. As of 2018, the Chinese government owns ALL the pandas, and no one can buy or sell them.

Natural predators of the *cub* pandas are [jackals], snow leopards, and [yellow-throated martens]. The adult giant panda is much harder for predators to capture and kill, so it has no real "wild" threats from predators.

Giant panda cubs are very fragile during the first weeks of their lives. They are tiny! They typically weigh from three to five *ounces* which is an unimaginable 1/900th of its mother's weight! Because they are blind and unable to crawl for up to two months, the mother sometimes accidentally crushes her infant. They are also hairless, so without their mother's care and protection from their natural predators, they would become very cold and could die. Their mother's milk is their only source of food in these {crucial} times of the giant pandas' lives. On the rare occasion, in the wild, that twins are born, the mother chooses the stronger of the two newborns to care for, and she abandons the weaker sibling.

In captivity, where twins are more common, humans' {intervention}, or help, usually manages to protect the lives of both babies. They keep the one the mother is *not* caring for at the time, in an incubator. Incubators are "machines" where animals are kept at the temperature they would be in the mothers' care.

Author's personal experience with such animal care... When pig litters were too big for their mother to safely give care, Dad built a fence in the hog house, and he kept the mother separated from her babies. He safely placed a heat light near the roof over the babies' side of the building. *Every* two hours, *day* and *night, Dad* would place one-half of the litter with the mother. When the babies had finished eating, he would put them back, get the mother up and help her lay back down on the other side. Then the next part of the litter was given their chance to eat. I remember, almost seventy years later, going with my dad a few times, to do this extremely demanding task. That personal experience clearly provides firsthand awareness for me, of the dedication zoo workers have in overcoming the challenges with which they are {confronted}.

Check for Understanding

2. What color are giant pandas?
3. What do you think is the meaning of endangered?
4+. Can you think of a time when you had a similar experience where someone worked REALLY hard to help a living thing survive? Perhaps it was not an animal. Maybe it was a special plant!

Research Suggestions

- What professions might you choose that could put you in a job that could help with the survival of a living thing?
- Where, specifically, could we go in the United States to see a living giant panda?

Activities

- Write a list of words from the story that you have learned. After you have researched something of interest to you about the giant panda, write a paragraph to share your new information. Try to correctly use some of the listed vocabulary in a way that provides {rich} text for YOUR readers.

F f

Family of Beavers

F f

Family of Beavers

The animal called "beaver" is a rodent. Beavers like to live on land and in the water. They are {semi-aquatic} herbivores. One of the two living species of beavers is native to North America. There is only *one* other rodent in the world larger than the beaver.

Sometimes, we see a beaver dam which might have caused a nearby pond to develop. As you read through this book, you will learn of another animal which is referred to as a "keystone species." That was a new term for my vocabulary (we are *all* learning). As I read about the beaver, I decided that it, too, is a keystone species. I can only include a *very* small part of the information about this incredible animal here, so I will suggest that you access resources to expand your own deeper knowledge. A trip to the library might also be a great outing!

Beavers use their rodent teeth to cut down trees. This drawing shows how long those "gnawing" teeth, which extend down below the lower lip, actually grow. Beavers prefer trees with [*diameters*] of two to six inches. They, however, have been known to {fell} trees of up to thirty-three inches, *almost three feet*, in diameter. It takes only a few minutes to cut down a small tree. For the bigger ones, beavers are intelligent enough to chew a certain depth, and then they just wait for some strong winds to finish their job. It is said that beavers can even decide which way they want the tree to fall. They cut it in a certain way that will make it fall where they want it! Beavers, which usually do their work at night, can change an entire habitat and favorably affect areas for the {sustainment} of many species of animals and plants.

Beavers don't waste a lot of their "lumber," as people often do. Beavers not only use their logs to dam up streams, and some rivers, but they also build their homes from the branches they weave and pack with mud to make them weather and waterproof. Beavers were even a *very positive* part in our history by the life-sustaining products these animals offered the Lewis and Clark expedition! A book titled *SEAMAN* is a good narrative about information on the expedition which includes information about the beavers.

The chewing of the tree itself, which is also a major food source for beavers, wears down their teeth which continue to grow throughout the life of the rodent. If rodents didn't gnaw on hard woody surfaces, the teeth would continue to grow so that they would pierce their jaw.

While the busy life of the beaver is important to many areas, it is also a {detriment} to others. According to Beaver Damage Management, the work of beavers can cause problems for utility companies in a variety of ways, which, in turn, can affect the lives of many people. Another far-reaching negative impact is the flooding that beaver dams can cause which could affect farmers' crop acres.

Some natural predators of beavers are coyotes, wolves, and mountain lions. However, their population is listed as "least concern" meaning that their population is stable.

Check for Understanding

2. What is the diameter of the trees beavers most prefer to cut down?
3. How do you think beavers were helpful on the Lewis and Clark expedition?
4+. How do you think humans could work with beavers to naturally create places that their effects would be valuable to people and other life on earth?

Research Suggestions

- What is a keystone species?
- What domestic animals, (pets), need to have hard things on which to chew?
- What is the name of the rodent which is larger than a beaver? Where would it be found in its natural habitat? Find that place on your world atlas that is in your binder.

Activities

- Draw the diameter of the **preferred** size of tree beavers gnaw to cut.
- Draw the diameter of the larger size mentioned above.
- In your spiral, draw another rodent that would need to gnaw on hard things. Show it chewing on its object.
- For the very proficient learner: Rewrite the descriptive paragraphs about the beaver. Be certain to have a clear introductory paragraph with the main idea. Supporting paragraphs need to have a topic sentence with supporting details. The closing sentence should refer back to the introduction.

G g

Group of Guinea Pigs

G g

Group of Guinea Pigs

The animal called "guinea pig" is a rodent. Guinea pigs typically live in the wild on the continent of South America. They originated in the Andes Mountains. The guinea pig is *not* native to the country of Guinea *nor* is it biologically related to pigs. No one really knows why they have the name guinea pig.

Guinea pigs live about four to eight years. They weigh between 1.5 and 2.6 pounds. If you have not converted from decimals to fractions, check in the back of this book for an *example*.

Write the fraction form of these weights in your spiral. If you have learned about the "lowest common denominator," write that fraction in your answer, too.

The adult guinea pig measures about eight to ten inches in length. Use your ruler to draw a [horizontal] line in your spiral to show the longest approximate length of an adult guinea pig. Draw along that line, again, until you reach the minimum, or shortest length, the adult guinea pig might grow. Make a little mark here. The ranges of those two lines would "hold" the adult guinea pig!

The teeth of a guinea pig continually grow and can only be kept at a healthy length by their gnawing on hard materials to wear them down. There are other animals in this book that have this same characteristic. Watch for those animals and list them in your spiral.

Guinea pigs sleep only about one-sixth of a twenty-four-hour day. How many hours are they *awake*? Hint: This is a two-part solution to find the answer. First, find how many hours they sleep by finding how many hours one-sixth of twenty-four equals. Then subtract the "quotient"—that is the name of the answer to a division problem—from twenty-four hours. The "difference," or the answer to a subtraction problem, is how long they are awake. Again, if you do not know how to divide this problem, check the back for an *example*.

Be sure to learn the correct names for the answers to division problems (quotient) and subtraction problems (difference). That will be required information in your math classes, if it is not already expected.

Check for Understanding

2. Where did the guinea pig first live? Find the words in the text and write them in your spiral.

3. Being able to do the first part with a ruler is significant. If the learner cannot do it, more instruction is needed and the provider can find ways to extend this outside the confines of this book.

4+. Being able to read and complete the two-step problem about sleep/wake time is sufficient proof of understanding.

Research Suggestions

- Through what countries and on what continent do the Andes Mountains extend?
- What research for treatment of a human medical condition involves guinea pigs? Name one.
- What do wild guinea pigs eat?
- Where was the most recent discovery of a new species of rodent that DOES NOT have the ability to gnaw or chew?

H h

Horde of Hamsters

H h

Horde of Hamsters

The animal called "hamster" is a small mammal. It is a rodent. Hamsters like to live in warm, dry areas, like [steppes], sand dunes, and the edges of deserts. Syria, a country in the Middle East region of the world, is where hamsters were first discovered in 1797. The golden or Syrian hamsters are the type of hamsters that are most commonly kept as pets. Hamsters also live in the wild in northern China, Romania, and Belgium.

Black-bellied hamsters live in the wild across France. They are rather [fierce] animals. There are only five hundred to one thousand remaining. They could become {extinct}. Black-bellied hamsters are {crepuscular}, which means they are most active during periods where there is some, but not much, light. They are most active just before sunrise and just after sunset. They stay hidden underground during the daytime when {diurnal} predators would be likely to catch them. Some natural predators of wild hamsters are snakes, mammals, and birds which catch small animals for food. These little animals defend themselves with their big [incisors] which are their most obvious rodent feature. The mothers will put the babies in the pouches in their mouths and run away to hide.

Depending on the species, hamsters measure from two and one-fourth to four and one-fourth inches, *up* to thirteen and a half inches. A short tail adds another two and a half inches.

Hamsters are omnivores in the wild. Like domesticated hamsters, they eat seeds, grains, and nuts among other things. In the wild, insects, frogs, and lizards are among their prey. The hamsters use those same pouches, where the babies are protected, to carry food back to their burrows.

Hamsters have poor eyesight. They are nearsighted and color blind so they can become visually confused. They are sensitive to movement around them. That is a main source of protection.

Their sense of smell helps hamsters find their food. They also can find and recognize their own babies using the scent of the infants.

The upright position of the hamsters' ears helps them with sound. They learn to recognize noises. As pets, they can tell when and where food is by its sound in the container. Hamsters also learn to recognize their owners' voices.

As with any future pet which you might be planning to acquire, be certain to learn all about them and their needs. Foods and temperature of their surroundings are just two important things to know.

Check for Understanding

2. In what country were hamsters first discovered in the wild? Read aloud the words that tell you that your answer is correct.
3. Do you think black-bellied hamsters will survive, or do you think that they will become extinct? Why do you think as you do?
4+. Knowing what wild hamsters eat, what effect do you think it would have on the country-side habitats of France if the black-bellied hamster were to become extinct?

Research Suggestions

• What are the important things that everyone who is thinking of getting a pet hamster should know? Be specific about each concern.
• Are hamster mothers always protective of their young?
• How do you think scientists know that hamsters are color blind?

Activities:

• Look at the drawing. Draw your own picture to place in your binder. Write a story about your hamster in your spiral. Include some of the information you learned from the paragraphs in the text.
• Find in your atlas the countries named in the text about hamsters.

I i

Implausibility of Gnus

I i

Implausibility of Gnus

The animal called "gnu," /new/, is a hoofed mammal. It is the largest species of antelope. Gnus are related to cattle, sheep, and goats. Gnus typically live in the wild, in the central [savannas] and plains in the southern and eastern parts of the continent of Africa, from Kenya to Namibia /nuh-mib-ee-uh/. The largest populations are found in the Serengeti in Tanzania /tan-zuh-nee-uh/ and Kenya. The gnu can also be found in dense [bush] and open woodland flood plains. This location is perfect for their needs as an herbivore because of the abundant growth of grass. When grass is not available they will eat leaves.

The gnu is also called a wildebeest. As the drawing shows, they have a mane, a beard, and curved horns. They also have a long tail. Measured at the shoulder, gnus range in height between forty-five and fifty-five inches. They weigh between three hundred and six hundred pounds. Their bodies are from five to eight feet in length, and their long tail is from fourteen to twenty-two inches.

As many as five hundred thousand gnu *calves* are born at the beginning of the [monsoon] season. There is a very high mortality rate, and only their own physical health, with the help of a very experienced mother, gives hope of survival.

Over 1.2 million gnus, or wildebeests, journey in a clockwise pattern over 1,800 miles each year to find better food and water supplies. As many as two hundred thousand zebras and gazelles make the trek with them. The other herbivores need the nourishing resources at the end of the journey, *and* this massive migration offers the most protection from their predators. Because of the numbers of animals, the lion population is intimidated to a point where young giraffes benefit from the protective presence also. The huge numbers make it less likely for single animals or small, more vulnerable groups to be attacked. However, during the migration, about 6,500 gnus drown while crossing the Mara River. The balance of nature in a healthy environment makes use of what could seem to be a tragedy. The carcasses that decompose add huge amounts of nutrients to the ecosystem in those areas. Local living organisms and animals are nourished by these remains.

Surprisingly, to me, was the fact that all of this trampling inflicted on the land and vegetation actually helped the ecological system. Rather than depletion of plant growth from trampling and excessive grazing, the millions of hoofs moving over the land stimulates the GROWTH of the grasslands! The [dung] that they leave behind that would also work into the soil with the foot traffic would be a tremendous natural fertilization as well.

Some natural predators of the gnu are lions, hyenas, African wild dogs, cheetahs, leopards, and crocodiles. When gnus suspect danger, they make a groaning call, and the entire implausibility stampedes away from the danger.

Check for Understanding

2. On what continent do gnus live in the wild? Find that continent in your world atlas.
3. What would a gnu probably be doing that would make it [vulnerable] to a crocodile?
4+. Can climate change have a negative effect on the gnu population? Why do you believe as you do?

Research Suggestions

*   Are gnus ever domesticated? If they are, for what purpose?
*   Do gnus serve any other purpose for the people where they live?

Activities

*   Write your research findings in your spiral. Use at least three complete sentences for each question. Be sure to use capital letters and punctuation appropriately.
*   Find the countries of Namibia and Kenya on the map of Africa in your world atlas.

J j

Journey of Giraffes

J j

Journey of Giraffes

The animal called "giraffe" is a mammal. Giraffes typically live on the continent of Africa. The best place to see large "herds" or journeys of giraffes is Kruger National Park in Africa.

Giraffes are earth's tallest living [terrestrial] animals, and they are the largest {ruminant}. The two horns on the top of their heads are sometimes used for fighting. They have an even number of toes, and they chew their [cud]. Domesticated cows in the United States also chew their cud.

Author's personal note: Mom had told me, when I was growing up on our farm, that if a cow "lost its cud," meaning that it could not {regurgitate} so that it could chew its food a second time, Dad would "feed" it a greasy dishrag. This would cause the cow to "vomit" and "find" its cud. The crisis had ended, and our very valuable cow would live! Since that time, veterinarians are well equipped with other current means to treat such an issue, and *I in no way recommend* doing what my dad did to solve such a serious problem!

When our grandchildren were quite young, a [docent] gave our family a visit behind the scenes at a local zoo, and they were able to feed a *very tall* giraffe. If you are able to visit a zoo, be sure to check out the beauty of these animals which are wonderfully and accurately depicted in the drawing on the *upper right side* of this page.

Giraffes are herbivores. These giant animals can eat hundreds of pounds of leaves in just one week's time! In the wild, the very long neck allows them {access} to the tops of the mimosa and acacia trees where they {retrieve} seeds, leaves, fruits, buds, and branches.

The natural predators of the giraffe are lions, leopards, spotted hyenas, and African wild dogs. Journeys of giraffes are composed of related females and their "children," *or* herds of adult males that have no family ties. Since giraffes are sociable animals, these types of journeys will gather together, which would help protect them from those dangerous animals that need them for their food, if *those* predators are able to survive.

Check for Understanding

2.   How tall are giraffes compared to other land animals?

3. Why is it important that we have zoos where the safe care of wild animals allows us to see them when most of us would never have the opportunity?

4+. Of what significance is it that an animal half way around the world could become extinct?

Research Suggestions

- How is the stomach of a ruminant different from the stomach of most other animals?
- What are other issues that are causing the endangerment of giraffes?

Activities

- Draw a diagram of the stomach of a ruminant. Then draw a diagram of the stomach of a human. Compare the two. Label the parts of each stomach. Put your diagrams in your binder.
- Verbally explain how the stomach of a ruminant {FUNCTIONS}.

K k

Kaleidoscope of Butterflies

K k

Kaleidoscope of Butterflies

The animal called "butterfly" is an insect. When counted, it appears that monarchs have only four legs. The last pair of legs curls and does not look like the other four legs. Butterflies, which are cold-blooded animals, typically live on six of the seven continents, {excluding} Antarctica.

A kaleidoscope is a continually changing pattern of shapes and colors. A movement of butterflies is a living example of a kaleidoscope. The orange wings of the monarch butterfly have black lines running through them. The wings are outlined with white dots. Millions of monarchs migrate south in the [autumn] from Canada and the northern part of the United States to California and Mexico. They would appear as a *giant kaleidoscope*. Humans can only see them up to a few hundred feet above the earth. Butterflies have actually been seen flying as high as eleven thousand feet en route to their winter destination. Few people would be in a position to see those magnificent sights.

There are four distinct stages in a monarch butterfly's life. They are the egg; the larva, or caterpillar; the pupa, or chrysalis; and the adult. They also go through *four generations* in a single year.

During the lifetime of a female monarch, which is about two to six weeks, she lays from one hundred to three hundred eggs on the underside of milkweed leaves. If she is the fourth generation of the single year's span, she will live from eight to nine *months*.

It takes only about four days for the EGGS to hatch into the second stage called the *larvae*. The larvae grow from less than one centimeter to about five centimeters, as they molt or shed their skin several times. While the larvae are attached to the leaf of the plant, they consume the leaf and ingest poisons that will stay in their bodies for their entire lifetimes. The caterpillars, or larvae, stop eating. They hang upside down from twigs or leaves using their last pairs of "prolegs" and spin a silk mat as they become *chrysalises*, the third stage of the life of the monarch. The third stage lasts for about seven to ten days before the final stage emerges as the *adult* monarch butterfly.

Check for Understanding

2. What kind of animal is a monarch butterfly?

3. When most animals do NOT emerge as an ADULT, why is the emergence of the monarch the ADULT?

4+. Why is it so important that the species does not become extinct?

Research Suggestions

- Does any stage of the monarch butterfly have a memory?
- What is the very unusual {phenomenon} or happening during the chrysalis stage?

L l

Lamentation of Swans

L l

Lamentation of Swans

The animal called "swan" is a bird. Swans typically live in the Northern Hemisphere, but some live in Australia, New Zealand, and South America. Most swans are found on lakes and rivers in the northern [contiguous] United States, Canada, and Alaska.

The trumpeter swan, the species which breeds in Michigan in the United States, is the world's largest species of waterfowl. It is the largest of the duck and goose "family." It stands four and a half feet tall and has a wingspan in excess of seven feet. It can grow to the weight of thirty pounds during its lifetime which can be from twenty to thirty years. The long, curved neck of the snow-white animal adds to its striking beauty, which calls attention to its desired wetland habit. Because people want to protect the swan and its surroundings, many other less known or recognized animals which share the areas are also protected.

The female, called a **pen**, is the mate that {incubates} the clutch of eggs. She lays from three to eight eggs in one nesting. The **cob**, or male, swims in the water surrounding the nest of stems and leaves of cattails and other aquatic plants to protect his growing family. The nest can be seen at the top of a muskrat house, or a beaver lodge, where it will stay above water level. It is in less danger from its land-based predators. The eggs are laid one at a time, and incubation does not begin until the last egg is laid. The **cygnets** will then hatch within a twenty-four-hour period, usually in midmorning. The male continues his ferocious defense of the lamentation as he fends off the swans' natural predators which prey on the younger members of the family. Included in that list are coyotes, minks, bald eagles, great horned owls, and snapping turtles. The additional predators of the larger of the animals are bobcats, otters, and human poachers who are illegally hunting the swans. Besides the actual predators, significant numbers of swans die from ingesting lead contained in fishing tackle equipment and ammunition.

Swans do not have teeth, but their serrated beaks are very necessary when they eat. While adult swans prefer vegetation for their food source, the cygnets, unlike other members of the bird population, must feed themselves from the beginning of their lives. If you get to watch a young family of swans, you may see the adults rocking to and fro (back and forth) in the water. Their feet are stirring up the silt at the bottom of the shallow water so that the cygnets can catch the tiny animals that they use to feed themselves.

The young swans begin to "fledge" or fly at about three to four months of age. During that time period, many of the deaths are caused by contact with power lines. Young swans stay with their parents through the first winter, but then they go out on their own.

In the 1930s, there were only sixty-nine swans known to be living in the United States, and they were all in the state of Montana. When Alaska became a state, more swans were found. Despite the percentage of deaths in the first three years of a swan's life, they are considered of "least concern" for endangered species.

Check for Understanding

2. What kind of animal is a swan?
3. What would happen to the cygnet if the cob was not with it?
4+. Where would swans be safest during the first three years of their lives?

Research Suggestions

- How do swans use their natural environment to build their nests to protect the cygnets when they hatch?

Activities

- From your research, draw a picture of the swan's nest and its base.
- Write a paragraph to explain your drawing. Edit your writing. Show any corrections in the blank space ABOVE each error.

M m

Memory of Elephants

M m

Memory of Elephants

The animal called "elephant" is a mammal. Elephants live in their natural habitats in Africa and Asia. Elephants are herbivores. The drawing here is one of the African elephants. The African bush elephant is *the largest* land animal living today! It is larger than the forest elephant that lives in wooded areas of Africa. The forest elephant is larger than their Asian cousin. The ears of the Asian elephant are smaller and shaped differently. Because the environment of the African elephant is much hotter, their very large ears help to make their bodies cooler. The size gives a broader surface for the animals' heat to "leave their bodies." Forest elephants are the major species targeted by ivory poachers. Their tusks, which are straighter and point downward, are more dense and are preferred by those who carve the ivory tusks.

Elephants also share some common characteristics. Most elephants have tusks which are super long incisor teeth. The prehensile snout, called a "trunk," is actually the extended growth of their nose and their upper lip. This unique body part is very important to the elephants. It is totally flexible, and the elephant can wrap it around things to move them. It is like an ultragiant straw because the elephants suck water up into it and then squirt it into their mouths so they can drink. It also provides the elephants with their greatest sensation which is the sense of smell. They can even smell water up to twelve miles away. African elephants' annual migration during the dry season, from June to November, leads them through thirty-seven of the fifty-four countries recognized by the United Nations today. They make this long and difficult journey to find water.

The oldest female is the leader of her memory of elephants. The {matriarch}, as the leader is called, can remember which animals are friends and which are enemies of her memory. They can remember where they have found food and water in the past. The elephant family unit is in constant {flux}, even during a routine day, but the memory is typically composed of the matriarch, young mothers, and their offspring, along with sisters, aunts, and cousins.

Other examples of the higher level of intelligence of elephants are many. A few are as follow.

- Elephants can recognize someone who has hurt them in the past by recognizing fabric by sight and smell.
- They can show grief when they find the remains of a dead animal. They have been seen gently touching those remains with their trunks and feet.
- They have been found to help other species, including humans, when they were in bad situations.
- They use their trunk as a tool for various jobs, including moving large tree trunks and limbs.
- A video was recently on national news when the Henry Doorly Zoo in Omaha, Nebraska, reached out to the local community after a wind storm had toppled trees and broken branches. The act had a twofold purpose: help clean up the community while providing free food for the elephants at the zoo. The video showed the animals using their trunks to carry away the piles of "food" to other parts of their artificial surroundings. Their trunks are used for many other challenges in their wild {habitats}.

Elephants are considered a {"keystone" species}. Using their natural physical capabilities for survival, they can turn a savanna into grasslands when uprooting trees and undergrowth to use them as part of their diets. They can create watering holes in dry land by digging with their trunks, tusks, and feet. The watering holes provide for the needs of the elephants as well as other animals living in the area.

Check for Understanding

2. What, specifically, is the largest land animal living today?
3. Why is "memory" a good collective noun for elephants?
4+. What would happen to the other animals if the elephants were not sharing their environment during the dry season?

Research Suggestions

- What would happen to their ecosystems if elephants no longer existed?
- Find other animals that have prehensile "parts." List the animal and its part in your spiral under an appropriate heading. Be certain that you are putting additions such as these in your spiral table of contents.
- What are the countries through which the elephants migrate?

Activities

- Using the most recent world atlas publication that you can find (that may be the one in your binder), locate the countries on the continent of Africa through which memories of elephants travel in their quest for water sources. List those in your spiral with an appropriate heading.

- If you can find a map of Africa showing the countries prior to 1980, circle any countries on the above list that you find on the older map. Draw a line through any that were not on the map.
- Write the names of the countries that have neither a circle nor a line. When were those countries established and why?

N n

Nide of Pheasants

N n

Nide of Pheasants

The animal called "pheasant" is a type of [fowl] which are birds that are commonly used for food.

Pheasants typically live in weedy fence rows, ditch banks, or brushy woods so they can have safe

cover from predators. "Birds that are hunted and used for human consumption such as turkeys and

pheasants are called *game* fowl. They *do not live in water*, although they do prefer to be near marshes

rather than really dry or arid places.

Common pheasants, also called ring-necked pheasants, were native to China and East Asia. They were brought to the state of Oregon in the United States in 1881. The fowl survived the ocean travel to the port in Washington State. Many did not survive the trip from Washington to Oregon. The roads were {treacherous} for the vehicles hauling the cargo. It took second and third additions to the original nides of pheasants before they really began to populate the area. They are now found in forty of the fifty states in the United States. Their meat is served in restaurants. For those who prefer to not hunt their own game, pheasant meat can be purchased in the grocery stores. Many farmers in the United States raise pheasants as their agricultural produce.

This breed of pheasant prefers to be on the ground, but they are excellent when flight is needed for safety. They are typically healthy birds that are active in the wild. The male, or *cock*, has a very different appearance than its female mate, which is called a *hen*. The adult male has a mass of 2.6 pounds and the female typically weighs 2 pounds. One of nature's ways of helping the birds protect themselves from becoming part of an endangered list is the vivid coloration of the cock. The bright colors distract predators from the more camouflaged colors of the hen.

She lays the eggs in nests made of grass, leaves, and weeds. The clutch size of the pheasant is eight to fifteen eggs. Incubation lasts for twenty-three to twenty-eight days. No more than two broods as young families of a female are called are hatched during one mating season. The hen provides care for the *chicks*. Chicks can fly by about twelve days of age but spend the first ten to twelve weeks with their mothers. The male has more than one mate. The cock beats his wings fiercely as he makes a loud crowing call to fend off predators from his brood. Natural predators include foxes, coyotes, owls, and hawks. Raccoons and skunks eat the pheasant eggs.

Pheasants like the farmers' harvested grain fields that provide much of their food for winter consumption. Summer food sources for wild pheasants include roots, berries, spiders, earthworms, and snails. The *chicks*, which must find their own food at a very young age, usually are ground feeders but are known to sometimes find sources in trees. Wildlife habitat management can help protect the pheasant population.

Check for Understanding

2. Name two of the surroundings that ring-necked pheasants like.
3. Why would the road travel from Washington State to Oregon cause many pheasants to die?
4+. What do you think about animals and plants being introduced to environments that are not natural for them? Discuss why it might be good (pros), and why it could be a bad (cons) decision.

Research Suggestions

- Learn about where in China the ring-necked pheasant lives. Compare the living conditions there to those in the northwest region of the continental United States. Consider climate, habitats, landforms, etc.

Activities

- Write a paragraph to record your research findings. You can locate some of the areas you will research in your binder atlas.

O o

Obstinacy of Buffalo

O o

Obstinacy of Buffalo

The animal called "*buffalo*" is one of one hundred species of hoofed mammals. Buffalo should not be confused with their distant cousin of the United States, the bison, which are commonly incorrectly named. True buffalo typically live on the continents of Africa and Asia. Their preferred sources to graze are tall grasses and short shrubs. They thin out dense grasses and reveal more types of foliage. Their exceptional swimming skills will take them through deep water to find better areas for food.

The very dangerous Cape buffalo is said to have a memory of someone years after they have been threatened and reportedly will seek revenge. When they are seeking such retribution, they give no warnings and simply ambush their "prey."

It is not uncommon for birds called oxpeckers to be found on the backs of the huge animals. These creatures have a {symbiotic} relationship which means both animals benefit from that relationship. The four-legged, split-hoofed mammal is rid of the annoying ticks and insects that {embed} themselves in the skin of the buffalo. The birds ride around on the backs of the buffalo and harvest their meals of the {parasites}.

When the obstinacy of buffalo, which usually numbers between fifty and five hundred, is searching for food and water, the pathfinders, as the *experienced cows* are called, lead them to their destinations. During the rainy season in the [Serengeti], the obstinacies can gather into the thousands of members.

Buffalo **cows** give birth to their first **calves** when the mother is about four or five years of age. The calves are in complete need of their mothers for the entire first year of their lives. If there is a threat from a predator, the adults face outward from the circle that they form around the young members of the gang (another collective noun for buffalo). The adults lower their heads and form a protective barrier using the horns that are visible in the drawing.

Lions, leopards, hyenas, and African wild dogs are among the wild dangers. The predators mainly attack the old, [infirm], or young defenseless populations. The adult buffalo can typically protect themselves in normal situations.

Check for Understanding

2. What do buffalo prefer to eat?
3. What could happen to the buffalo if the oxpeckers were not there?
4+. How do you think animals know how to do the kinds of things they do to protect their young?

Research Suggestions:

- Are buffalo important to native people in any way?
- Are buffalo ever domesticated?

P p

Prickle of Porcupines

P p

Prickle of Porcupines

The animal called "porcupine" is a rodent. Porcupines typically live in forests, grasslands, and desert shrub areas, as well as [tundra], on the North American continent. They *are* found on *every* continent with the exception of Antarctica.

Porcupines are not particularly social animals, so they tend to [forage] alone. They are herbivores, and they feed on bark, stems, nuts, [tubers], seeds, grass, leaves, fruit, and buds. They do not eat meat, but they do chew on the bones of dead animals. The chewing not only sharpens their teeth, but the substance from the bones also adds minerals, such as salt and calcium, to their diet.

The prehensile tail of the porcupine adds to its balance as it moves through trees grasping branches as it goes. It also hangs upside down to place its front feet in position to reach out for its food. The porcupines have poor eyesight, but their senses of touch, hearing, and smell are their best assets.

Natural predators that kill porcupines, including lynx, coyotes, wolves, and great horned owls, to name a few, do so by attacking and biting their unprotected faces. Their predators also flip them over to expose the prickly animals' soft and unprotected underbellies.

The North American porcupine is the only species found in the United States and Canada. They are pests to humans in many ways, but one of the greater concerns is the fact that they can carry many diseases including rabies. They are [host] animals to ticks which can spread Colorado tick fever.

The mother porcupine and her ***porcupettes***, which are born with soft quills that harden in just a few days, comprise the prickle. Porcupettes are usually born between April and June and, depending on the species, mature in nine months to two and a half years. There are typically one to three babies born at a time. Several groups of offspring can be born to that mother in one year's time. The rodents are known to live up to fifteen years in the wild.

Porcupines are second only to the beaver in size in North America. The reddish orange appearance of their front teeth is due to iron oxide in the tooth enamel that strengthens their teeth for gnawing on branches and trees. As with other rodents about which you have read in this book, those teeth continue to grow throughout their lifetimes.

Porcupines are intelligent animals that are quick to learn, and they possess good memories. This helps them know when to [employ] their some thirty thousand quills, each of which has between seven hundred and eight hundred barbs. While not poisonous, their skin-piercing sharpness is quite painful. The tale that porcupines can shoot their quills at their enemies is untrue, but they do come off easily. They can attach to a predator that comes too close. Porcupines have also been known to run sideways or backward into their predators, allowing those quills to lodge in the [potential] attackers' flesh. They can also swing their tails into the predators. The unique pungent odor that porcupines {exude} also lets predators know the quills are raised and ready for "combat."

Another problem that porcupines cause can also be a benefit. They do tremendous damage to young trees. The marks they leave on trees with their long sharp teeth can measure up to five millimeters wide. While this damage is NOT welcome in most situations, porcupines evolved with the forests and helped in forest [replenishment]. The trees these animals damage become a much-needed habitat for many other species of animals. As the damaged trees decay, they become part of the nutrients for living trees and other forest vegetation. Thinning the growth helps other trees by also giving them more space and nutrients.

Check for Understanding

2. How many quills does the North American species of porcupines have?
3. What would happen to the porcupettes if the mother died? Explain your answer.
4+. What would have been the effects on earth's environment if the porcupines had not "evolved with the forests"?

Research Suggestions

- How do the predators "digest" the animal?
- What other rodent, besides the beaver, is larger than porcupines?
- Where does it live?

Activities:

- Draw an illustration of the animal that is larger than the porcupine.
- Determine the size of each of those three largest rodents.
- Use your ruler to draw lines to show their heights in order.
- Label each measurement with the animal's corresponding name.

Q q

Quarrel of Sparrows

Q q

Quarrel of Sparrows

The animal called "sparrow" is a bird which is actually considered a reptile! (Another example of my own learning as I am creating this book!) The house sparrow actually originated in the Middle East region of the world and spread beyond in every direction. They typically lived in most of Europe, the Mediterranean Basin, and much of Asia. They were brought to North America from Europe in the 1800s. It is not known whether it was an intentional move. If you recall reading the entry about the business of ferrets, the European ferret was intentionally introduced in the 1600s to the British American colonies in what is now the Northeast region of the United States.

The house sparrow, shown in the drawing to the right, is one of the species commonly seen in cities and on farms in the United States. During colder weather, they are found from Southern Canada, across the United States, and through Central America. In the summer, they extend northward to Southern Alaska.

The male of the species is chunky in size, with a large head, barrel chest, a short neck, and short legs. The tail is medium in length. The bill is short and cone shaped. The very pointed end helps the animal pick up the tiny grains and seeds, such as millet. They also eat insects and discarded human food. They are drawn to bird feeders with store-bought mixtures. They enjoy eating and are very messy. They are not very welcome close to houses and outside living areas. Sparrows are very social and tend to create noisy chirping flocks. They are also aggressive toward other feeder birds and will force the others away from the food. Perhaps the last two sentences provide the basis for their collective noun, "quarrel" of sparrows.

It is easy to distinguish between the male and female by appearance. The male, shown in this drawing, is brown and gray, and it has a black mask across the eyes. The female does *not* have the black mask. They are also tan and brown with a pale line back from the eye.

Check for Understanding

2. Find the words in the above text that tell where in the world sparrows originated.
3. What would be some ways to ensure that the sparrows have access to foods they may need, while protecting the less aggressive feeder birds?
4+. Why is it important to realize that even the sparrow is a living thing?

Research Suggestions

- What are the predators and prey in the lives of the house sparrow?
- Do house sparrows ever present any serious problems for humans?

Activities

- Look for sparrows in your surroundings.
- Look for any other birds that you might see.
- Keep a "diary" in your spiral about those sightings.

R r

Rangale of Deer

R r

Rangale of Deer

The animal called "deer" is a mammal. Deer typically live in wetlands, [deciduous] forests, grasslands, rain forests, [arid] [scrublands], and mountains. They are considered *generalists* which means they are *able* to adapt to a wide range of habitats. The distance they live within is determined by the *quality of the environment* to provide for their needs. If *plentiful* amounts of *food* and *water* are available, they require *less space* and may need no more than a *square mile* of "home space." They prefer to make their sleeping areas where tree and [underbrush] growth provides for natural protection from the elements and potential predators.

White-tailed deer are known to eat over six hundred different plants. The sharp incisors allow deer to tear through very tough plants. Their four-chambered stomach is formed so that the deer merely swallow the plants and cough them back up after grazing is completed. The deer then grind the plants with their very large molars before swallowing again for the digestion process. In the summer, deer eat the foods available to them. These foods, much to the dislike of the farmers, include crops of soybeans and corn. In the wild, they eat berries, fungi, nuts, *and they* love the fresh apples and pears from *my backyard* fruit trees while providing beautiful entertainment for me! In winter, when they stay closer to the wooded areas for protection from the weather, they feed on bark and twigs from the trees.

There are a variety of growth descriptions for the antlers of the whitetails. When the rack begins as part of the skull extension, very small protrusions still under the skin on the head emerge. These animals are referred to as "button" bucks. Antlers grow at a very fast rate. Some deer antlers even grow at a rate of *one inch* per *day*! The racks found on deer have distinctive points called tines. The length and number of tines an adult male **buck** grows each year are determined by the *nutrition*, *genetics*, and the *age* of each animal. Each spring, the antlers get their blood supply from a velvety covering. When the rack has reached full maturity, the deer rub against trees to remove the now-use-less substance. The rack hardens and remains throughout the fall until the deer "shed" them in the winter. The shed rack becomes a welcome supply of nutrients for the rodents including mice, chipmunks, squirrels, and even porcupines that live in the forests. They can sharpen their teeth, and they can also wear down those ever-growing teeth so that they do not grow back into the owner's body.

When the female *doe* reaches maturity, her first offspring is one single *fawn*. After that, she usually gives birth to twins, and sometimes triplets, each mating season. *Very rarely* have *does* been known to have four *fawns* at one time. Most fawns, born each year, do not survive until maturity.

The *doe* is the sole caregiver of the newborns. After nursing them, the mother leads her newborns into *her* safer home range habitat.

Due to the decrease in the population of bobcats, wolves, and coyotes which were the major predators of white-tailed deer, humans are now the only major predator for the animal.

Check for Understanding

2. What are two of the animals that consume some of the shed racks?
3. What other animals that you have read about in this book have a similar digestive system?
4+. What do you think the doe does with her fawns while she forages for her own food?

Research Suggestions

- When might a buck shed its antlers in the summertime?
- What about the structure of the eyes of deer causes them to see better at dawn and dusk than in the middle of the day?
- There is some controversy among those who hunt for the purpose of food consumption, those who hunt for sport, and those who think deer should NOT be hunted at all. Research the reasonings and support given for each position. Summarize your findings.

Activities

- If you have a study partner, have them do their own independent research. When information is secured, "draw straws" to see which side of the debate each of you will represent. Have an objective third person "judge" which debater gave the most clearly stated argument. If you have no study partner, ask your provider to assume that role. Ask another person to be the "judge."
- *After* the debate, decide if either of you changed your actual position.
- What is the current population trend concerning those wild predators of deer in your area?

S s

Study of Owls

S s

Study of Owls

The animal called "owl" is a bird. Owls typically live in many habitats and do not migrate during colder weather. There are two hundred different species of owls throughout the world, and the great horned owl, shown here, is the most common in all of North and South America. In fact, it is the one with which people are most familiar. You can sometimes hear the *whooo, whooo, whooo* call between owls in the dark of night. There have been no fossil remains of this particular species because of their ability to easily adapt to a wide variety of changing environments. Because of that, scientists know little about their history.

This particular bird of prey does NOT have horns, but the large ears do give the impression that they exist. The salt-and-pepper effect of the dark-gray and dark-brown feathers with some white ones randomly placed throughout their body covering makes them well camouflaged during the day when they are resting/sleeping. The composition of the feathers makes it the fastest of all owls. If need be, it can fly at the rate of forty miles per hour. It often flies about thirty miles an hour. The adaptation of these feathers which cover the great horned makes its flight silent. The adult female has an upright stance of twenty-five inches tall while the *smaller male* stands only twenty inches in height. The wing span is fifty to sixty inches.

The flat face of the great horned owl has the largest eyes of all the owl species in the entire world, and it has excellent vision. The size does not necessarily give it any better vision over others in its owl "family." The eyes are not "ball" shaped as most animals' eyes are. They are actually tube shaped, and they are *completely immobile.* That fact provides them with the ability to totally focus on their prey which includes insects, small mammals, and other birds. It also improves their depth perception. You can see by the drawing that the {talons} are very sharp and strong. This is a very important characteristic to aid them in capturing and killing their prey.

While there are more than one collective noun for owls which might encourage us to think that they are very social creatures, these nocturnal animals prefer to hunt alone. This owl's neck rotates or turns *270 degrees*! A straight line, _____, is 180 degrees.

Check for Understanding

2. What is the shape of the eyes of this owl? Think about the possible benefits and shortcomings of the phenomenon. Write at least three sentences for your answer.
3. Why would good depth perception be important for an owl?
4+. What is the geometric angle of the rotation of the head of the great horned owl? If you have a protractor or compass, draw that angle in your spiral. Label the angle.

Research Suggestions

- What is the group name for owls, most vultures, eagles, etc., that capture and kill their food?
- What species is the smallest measurement of owl in the world?
- What is the largest? Compare them to the great horned owl.
- What are the predators of the great horned owl?

Activities

- Draw lines to show those actual sizes of the smallest, largest, and great horned owl.
- Label them in order of size.
- Draw a representation of each of the three owls.

Troop of Kangaroos

Troop of Kangaroos

The animal called "kangaroo" is a {marsupial} mammal. A major characteristic of a marsupial is that the adult females have a pouch on their bellies where they carry their newborn. Kangaroos originally lived in eastern Australia, but they can be found on some of the islands near the "island/continent." Their natural habitats |vary| and include forests, woodlands, plains, and savannas. These habitats provide the {herbivore} with the plant foods they primarily use to survive. Because there is an increase in population in the wild, there is a concern that the natural habitat may not be able to support the large numbers of kangaroos.

Kangaroos are important to the [aboriginal] peoples of Australia. The natives of Australia see them as "{totem}" or a Creator Spirit, and therefore, kangaroos are sacred to the people.

Kangaroos' large feet and |very| strong hind legs make it possible for them to leap as far as thirty feet (nine meters) at one time. They can cross more than thirty miles in an hour's time. The strong tail provides the necessary balance during movement.

The kangaroo is the tallest marsupial, measuring over six feet (two meters) tall. If they are threatened, they pound the earth to give warning to their troop which Australians call mob. Kangaroos fight by using their powerful legs to kick. Sometimes, they resort to biting their opponents.

Joeys, as baby kangaroos are called, live, totally supported by their mothers, in the female's pouch. At about four months of age, the joey ventures outside to eat some grass and small shrubs, but it returns to the pouch for safety. By ten months of age, the maturing young kangaroo is able to live completely on its own without {nurturing} by its mother.

Humans and [dingoes] are the only real predatory threat to kangaroos. However, the vanishing habitat during heat and drought, which causes extreme hunger for the animals due to lack of plant growth, is also threatening to their existence. The massive fires which ravaged the south coast of Australia where kangaroo sanctuaries exist, have been {devastating} to the population there.

Check for Understanding

2. What kind of mammal is a kangaroo?
3. What is causing the food source of the kangaroo to disappear?
4+. How would you feel if something you hold sacred was not protected?

Research Suggestions

• What is being done to protect the habitat for the survival of the kangaroo?

U u

Unkindness of Ravens

U u

Unkindness of Ravens

The animal called "raven" is a bird. Ravens typically live across the northern hemisphere. According to one source, the collective noun, unkindness, is *very unfair*! They have been known to show empathy toward their "friends." They seem to console them if they lose in a fight. They *remember* who those friends are, and that memory has been noted to last for at least three years. Of course, the negative memories evoke negative reactions as well.

The *raven*, for me, has been one of the most difficult animals about which to write. Factual sources and information included such descriptions that made them seem unreal or from a fantasy narrative!

The intelligence of a raven reportedly ranks with that of the chimpanzees and dolphins. Ravens have retrieved food, dangling on string, during the first try. Some have completed that task in as little as *thirty seconds*! They also intentionally hold objects up for attention. They are great with body language when they communicate with each other. They use their beaks to point to objects just as humans use fingers to point to something in order to draw attention. Researchers say that these naturally occurring gestures have only been seen in primates!

Ravens, along with fellow birds such as song birds, crows, and jays, are ritualistic in using something called anting. Ants and ant carcasses are involved in creating something similar to an insecticide. They perform various activities to achieve their end goal, a more comfortable existence for themselves. I will leave the details of the more descriptive actual processes to your own research.

Native Americans describe ravens as mischievous. In Alaska and Canada, ravens have used snow-covered roofs as slides. They roll down snowy hills in Maine. They play keep-away with other animals like dogs and otters. Ravens make toys out of pine cones, rocks, sticks, etc. They use them to play by themselves or "with friends." Sometimes, they just mock and torment other animals for the fun of it.

In the wild, ravens "trick" other animals out of their food. One raven will distract the animal from enjoying a good meal while the other raven steals it. They have pushed rocks onto people to keep them from getting to their nests. They've stolen fish right off the fisherman's line that was submerged in a hole in the ice! They have been known to imitate wolves and foxes to get them to come to another dead animal to break open the carcass. The raven waits patiently while the mammal eats its fill. Then the scavenger moves in safely for the "left overs." They even "played dead" beside a beaver carcass to scare away other ravens. If they know another raven is watching them as they are trying to hide something, they will *pretend* to hide it and sneak it to another hiding place. That trick only works for so long, because *all* ravens are *smart*!

In captivity, ravens learn to talk even better than some parrots. They mimic car engines, toilets flushing, animal and bird calls, and more.

There are a number of mythical descriptions from worldwide cultures throughout very early world history! There are varying beliefs, but most seem to revolve around mystery and evil.

In a recent news article from England quoting a 2018 statement from the ravenmaster for the "Tower of London's Queen Raven," he agreed with the "camp" who finds ravens in a positive "light." He described the resident ravens in some of their daily behaviors: "Croaking loudly at visitors, posing for selfies, rifling through (visitors) bags looking for a box of Pringles…"

Then he specifically described Merlina, the raven which asserted herself as the "leader of the roost" after joining the small "unkindness" in 2007. She has been missing and presumed dead, since her habit of leaving the Tower Green for a short period of time and then returning to her home roost has not been reality this time.

Merlina would lie on her back on the Tower Green with her legs in the air, *playing* dead. Of course, those unfamiliar with her stunts were in shock.

In apparent refute of my earlier paragraph concerning "evil," the ravenmaster says, "But here the omen is a good omen. I see my role as educational. I am trying to educate visitors about how beautiful, and intelligent, and smart (the ravens) actually are."

One more sinister legend in England, has it that if there are fewer than six ravens at the tower, the kingdom will fall. Happily, for the country of England, there are still seven ravens at the tower. No rush to fill Merlina's vacancy are in the plans at this time. It is hoped that a **chick** from the raven "court" will be hatched which will be up to the task of "replacing" Merlina.

The close-up of the head in the drawing above which looks very much like the photo of Merlina, shows the very alert eye of this highly intelligent creature. That, in itself, makes all the above "antics" of the raven very believable! A closer look reveals bristle-like feathers extending down the beak. These function much like the nose hairs in the nostrils of humans. They act as filters, especially when the raven is flying. They keep dust and dirt out of the nares /NAY-reez/ and respiratory system. The external openings in the upper part of the bill let them breathe without opening their beak. Some other birds have this "organ" function, too. It is thought that the bristles may also help with the sensation of touching something.

Ravens, which mate for life and live in pairs, stay in their own territory. Their young leave "home" when they reach "adolescence." They join "gangs." They live and eat together until they mate and pair off. Scientists, who have studied these age groups, have determined that the "gang members" have a much higher level of stress. When they mate, as adults, that stress level seems to subside to a certain degree. Since there are few predators, the raven can live in the wild up to seventeen years. In captivity, that expectation is increased to forty years! Ravens can adapt to ANY environment. They can live in snowy areas as well as deserts. They are found in mountainous areas as well as forests. They are scavengers that eat fish, meat, seeds, fruits, carrion, and garbage. Ravens are definitely *omnivores*!

Check for Understanding

2. What do ravens eat?
3. Why does society need ravens to exist?
4+. Why do you think the bristle-like feathers on the ravens' beaks are an important part of their anatomy (body structure)?

Research Suggestions:

- Why are ravens kept at the Tower of London?
- Why are ravens so important that the government would hire a ravenmaster?
- What happens to the surviving raven when its mate is no longer with it?
- What are the predators of ravens?

V v

Venue of Vultures

V v

Venue of Vultures

There is some controversy concerning whether vultures should continue to be considered raptors and birds of prey. My sources stated the information which I have included here.

The animal called "vulture" is a [scavenging] bird of prey. {New World} vultures typically live in the western hemisphere from southern Canada to South America. The *turkey vulture* is one of twenty-six North American raptors, but it is not a bird of prey. Most vultures are strong enough, with feet that are equipped with sharp talons that can kill their prey and tear it apart to eat it. The turkey vulture *does not* have such capabilities. The advantages that turkey vultures do possess are a strong sense of sight and smell. The stronger and more aggressive black vultures take advantage of the turkey vultures and follow them on their pursuit of the {carrion} or {decomposing} meat that both need for food. The black vultures then force their [benefactors] from the dead animals.

There seems to be some disagreement as to the turkey vultures' position in the species membership. Some say that because the feet are more like that of a stork that they are not recognized as birds of prey. Others contend that they are vultures. The red bald head resembles that of the wild turkey so they are given their name based on that similarity. The bald head prevents fragments of the carrion from sticking to the feathers of the animal.

Contrary to past opinions about the turkey vultures, they are now valued for their contribution to the safer environments which they help to create from their desired diet of decaying flesh. Their food preference rids the local environments of the undesirable smell and unhealthy conditions created by the very food the turkey vulture eats. The fact that these birds cannot carry their food from where they find it causes them to be placed where they can be hit by motorists.

The population of this New World species numbers more than five million. In the areas where the VENUE of vultures roosts, the groups range from several birds to several hundred birds. As the venues migrate, they can grow in size to several thousand. Sizes increase significantly in tropical areas. Mexico and Central America find venues exceeding ten thousand vultures. When they travel, turkey vultures fly among the broad-winged hawk and Swainson's hawks.

The birds avoid heavy muscular work when flying by soaring and gliding on the thermal and mountain updrafts. They can be seen along mountain ridges, shorelines, and coastlines where these beneficial winds are more common. They avoid large bodies of water, and they do not fly in rain or during cloudy conditions because the updrafts are {suppressed}.

When the turkey vultures are too young to fly, the ***nestlings***, as they are called, defend themselves from their enemies by {projectile} vomiting, a forceful thrust which can travel a few feet toward their targets.

As full-grown adults, their wingspan has been measured to be five feet and six inches. The length of their body is from two feet and two inches to two feet and eight inches. Their weight ranges from three and a half to five pounds. In flight, wings in a "V" above their back help the animal to stabilize their bodies in {turbulent} winds.

The most northern of the species are the most active in migrations, while those living farther south do not tend to be as active. Small towns across the Midwest section of the United States can expect them back in the spring of the year.

Check for Understanding

2. What is one of the two senses that turkey vultures use to find their source of food?
3. What would happen to local environments if the turkey vultures were not there to devour the carrion?
4+. Why would the turkey vulture want to take advantage of the updrafts to help them travel?

Research Suggestions

- How many eggs are laid, and how many times a year are they laid?
- What are the predators of turkey vultures?
- Are there other unique ways that turkey vultures protect themselves?

W w

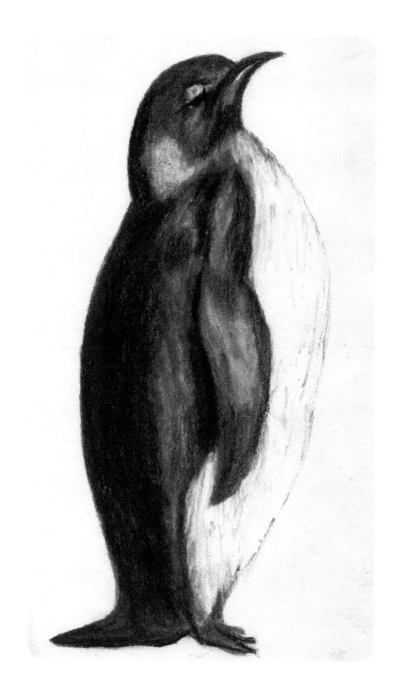

Waddle of Penguins

Waddle of Penguins

The animal called "penguin" is a {flightless} bird. Penguins typically live in earth's Southern [Hemisphere].

When penguins are on land, the collective noun is *waddle*. When they are in water, the term is *raft*.

Studies have shown that overweight penguins tend to have a "wobblier waddle." The rocking motion, as the animal waddles, helps raise their center mass so the muscles do not have to work so hard. Their legs are very short, so they must waddle. If the legs and body were shaped differently they could not dive and swim as well. Escape from their predators would be more difficult, and they would not be as successful in catching their prey. Penguins typically walk one or two kilometers per hour. When they are frightened, they can run much faster than a human could over snowy rocks and ice.

Penguins stopped flying millions of years ago. Their wings {transformed} into flippers which, along with their streamlined bodies, make them the fastest swimming, and deepest diving, species of any birds. They can stay underwater up to twenty minutes at a time.

The fact that the penguins can also drink seawater when they are in the ocean allows them to be excellent in their pursuit of their prey. Penguins are the predators of many different kinds of fish and other sea life. The inside of their toothless mouth is lined with back-facing fleshy spines which help guide the fish down the penguins' throats. Penguins spend about half of their time in water. The other half of their time is spent on land. When on land, penguins drink fresh water from puddles. They also eat snow.

The emperor penguin, {depicted} here, is the tallest and the heaviest of all of the living penguin species. It can measure from 3.6 feet to 4.3 feet in height. The male can weigh as much as fifty-one pounds. Their life span in the wild is approximately twenty years.

The emperor penguins nest in the winter. The female places a single egg on the top of the male's feet where the egg {incubates} in his brood pouch. The female goes off to the sea to feed on fish and other sea life. Her mate keeps the egg warm until she returns about sixty-five days later. The egg typically hatches a few days before the mother returns. Then the male, which has had *nothing* to eat, goes to feed. When he returns, both parents care for their ***chick***.

The emperor penguins' predators also include birds. Among them are the southern giant petrels which are responsible for about one-third of emperor chicks' deaths in some colonies. Penguins' main predators in the water include the leopard seal, fur seal, sea lions, sharks, and killer whales. On land, for the penguins that live in a somewhat warmer climate, snakes, lizards, and dogs like to eat their eggs and chicks.

Penguins are extremely intelligent and can be trained or conditioned. They communicate with each other, and they can even use tools. They form [intricate] communities and {hierarchies} which means animals have a line of importance in ranking, from the leader to the lowest responsibility of followers. Penguins do not like to be touched. If they feel threatened, they may bite with their sharp beaks that are like strong clamps.

The yellow-eyed penguin is one of the rarest of penguins. It has been on the endangered list since 1988. As of 2017, there were less than 3,700 still living in the wild on New Zealand's South Island.

Check for Understanding

2. How long can penguins stay under water?
3. After reading all of the information on this page, why do you think penguins might have stopped flying? Think about the habitat, sources of food, the size of the bird, etc.
4+. Since these animals live in the southern hemisphere, would their extinction affect the ecosystems of the northern hemisphere? Explain your answer and write it in your spiral.

Research Suggestions

- What are other species of flightless birds living today?
- What "chain reaction" involving climate change could cause the penguin populations to become extinct?

Xx

Create your own collective noun and its object.
Draw it in your spiral.

Xx

Write your own information that you want your audience to know about your "critter."

Y y

Yap of Chihuahuas

Y y

Yap of Chihuahuas

The animal called "Chihuahua" /chi/wa/wa is a mammal known as a small dog. Chihuahuas were typically found in the state of Chihuahua in the country of Mexico. Zeke, my grandniece's sweet, little, long-haired Chihuahua, is posing nicely in this portrait. His short-haired siblings are the typical vision that most of us who are familiar with the breed recognize. There are two official varieties of Chihuahuas: short and long haired. They are BOTH types of *one breed*. Chi's, as they are called, can live from fourteen to eighteen years. This is considered to be a very long life span in the {canine} "family" of mammals. The three leading causes of death are cardiovascular disease, [trauma], and infection.

It is claimed that [conquistadores] in Mexico found many of the small Chihuahuas in the sixteenth century. They became so popular that many of them were purchased and brought to the United States as pets. Midget was the first Chihuahua to be registered by the AKC (American Kennel Club) in 1904. Gidget was the Taco Bell mascot which appeared on the scenes in 1997.

A mother usually gives birth to no more than three ***pups***, although up to six have been recorded. Chihuahuas are the smallest of the purebred dogs. A little female named Milly was recognized in the Guinness Book of World Records in 2014. She earned the honor according to her height of 3.8 inches. The inclusion is based on height, not weight. Milly replaced Boo Boo, which had held the record at 4 inches. Boo Boo was a long-haired Chihuahua like Zeke, shown above.

Overfeeding Chihuahuas or feeding them the wrong types of food can lead to problems with bone development. Bone problems can include bone weakening or bowing, which is poor bone formation. Obesity, skin problems, and [rickets] can also be problems. If you are planning to get a pet of any kind, be sure to research everything about the animal before you purchase! The Internet has many sites where you can learn more.

Because of their size it is not wise to leave your Chihuahua outside unattended. Common predators are owls, hawks, and other large birds of prey. Chihuahuas, especially the short-haired variety, are also sensitive to cold temperatures.

Author's note: Since doing this research, my daughter actually acquired a rescue dog that is said to be Chihuahua. Her dog, Boston, is a short-haired type. He certainly looks like one in the face, but he may very well have a mix of breeds. Rescue dogs do not come with "papers," but they need love, too, and are very willing to give it back exponentially!!

I guarantee, from this recent reminder, *pet dogs* and their proper care *are definitely* time consuming and a *lot* of work. They are very well worth it if you have an appropriate home to give them and the time and energy to follow through with proper care!

Check for Understanding

2. What is the name of the dog in the portrait? Find it and write a sentence about him using his name. Be sure to use a noun in the subject of the sentence and an "active verb" in the predicate or the part of the sentence that follows the verb.
3. How could the second leading cause of the death of Chihuahua dogs be prevented?
4+. If cold temperatures negatively affect a Chihuahua, do you think extreme exposure to the sun could also be an issue? Explain your answer.

Research Suggestions

- What is a conquistador?
- Why were they in Mexico?
- How long ago were they there?
- What is the meaning of exponentially?

Activities

- Write a paragraph or two, in your spiral, describing the history of Mexico during the time when the conquistadors were there.
- Find and list the opinions in the story about Chihuahuas.

Z z

Zeal of Zebras

Z z

Zeal of Zebras

The animal called "zebra" is a mammal of the horse "family." Zebras typically live in the grasslands of Eastern and Southern Africa. They can survive in the wild up to twenty-five years. Zebras are herbivores, so their habitat is perfect for their needs. They like to eat tree bark, leaves, and grass. Like the horses that are common in parts of the United States, zebras have one solid hoof on each of four feet.

You can see from the drawing that zebras have a striped coat of white and black and/or brown. Zebras have black skin under white coats which have the stripes *on* the coat. The stripes provide the necessary camouflage when the zeal of zebras huddles together so that no individual zebra stands out alone. Zebra stripes are like human fingerprints because *no two* animals have the exact same patterns. Each of the three species has its own unique pattern of stripes. The Grevy's zebras' stripes are thin. Mountain zebras have vertical stripes on the neck and [torso]. Their [haunches] have horizontal stripes.

Some of the plains zebras, which are represented in the drawing on this page, have brownish stripes between their black stripes. There are more plains zebras, which are also called the common zebras, than either of its relatives. Plains zebras are the smallest of the three types. They can measure three and a half to fiive feet high, and adults can weigh between 386 to 849 pounds. The unique stripes of the plains zebra are broad stripes which run horizontally toward the back. The stripes that run toward the front are vertical. The horizontal and vertical stripes come together to form a triangle in the middle of their bodies. There is a stripe that runs down the center of their backs, along their spine, and it continues out onto their tails. Their stripes are also found on their underbelly.

The very good eyesight and hearing that zebras possess are significantly important senses to help the animals survive their natural predators. Lions, hyenas, leopards, and cheetahs are among those predators. The zebras' speed, up to thirty-five miles per hour, is also a survival resource. A zeal consists of small groups which include the male, called a ***stallion***; several female ***mares***, which also comprise the stallion's harem; and their young. When they encounter a dangerous animal, they let out a sharp "two-syllable" call. The female and the young run! The male follows them so that he can defend his families. If the predators come close enough, the zebra will meet them with a very powerful kick from his strong legs. If a member is actually attacked, other zebras will circle around the member to provide protection.

Zeals of zebras usually spend most of their days grazing on the grasses in their surroundings. Because of the need to grind that vegetation, their teeth in the back of their mouths are worn. Nature has provided the characteristic that is needed. Those back teeth continue to grow!

Like the "memories of African elephants," "zeals of zebras" must travel long distances to find food and water during dry seasons. They still need to sleep, but not without large groups to huddle together. They need the protection of the alertness of all the "zeals" to warn of approaching dangers.

Check for Understanding

2. To what specific animal "family" do zebras belong? Read the words in the text that tell you that.
3. What could happen if a few zebras were unable to travel from their home grasslands in dry weather? Try to think of two.
4+. What is a purpose for the zebras in their habitat of Southern Africa?

Research Suggestions

- Have zebras ever been domesticated?

Activities

- List, in your spiral, all of the animals in this book that have any teeth that continue to grow. As you write your answers, tell in what part of the mouth those teeth would be located.

Answers for Alphabetically Listed Animals

Beavers	buffalo	butterflies	
Chihuahuas			
Deer			
Elephants			
Ferrets	frogs		
Giraffes	gnus	guinea pigs	
Hamsters			
Kangaroos			
Owls			
Pandas	penguins	pheasants	porcupines
Ravens			
Seals	sparrows	swans	swine
Vultures			
Zebras			

What the learner determines for the letter *x* will possibly require adjustments for this answer sheet.

The letters with the most animals are *p* and *s*.

The letters with no animals are *a, i, j, l, m, n, q, t,* u, *w,* (*x*), and *y*.

Answers vary by learner's own creation of a collective noun for the letter *x*, and their imaginary animal OR their real animal which they chose for that collective noun.

Note: not all plurals are spelled by adding s or es. Example: The spelling of both buffalo and deer are used as either singular or plural. You must look to the verb before or after the word in question. If the sentence says, "The deer was in my back yard." *Deer* is singular. *Was* is a singular verb and is the clue to tell that there is one. If the sentence says, "There are deer in my backyard." *Deer* is plural. *Are* is plural and is the clue that there are more than one.

Some answers and possible answers to use as examples for questions in "ABCs" are as follow. Use these to determine the accuracy of what your learner is saying to answer the rest of the questions and their accuracy. Unless the question is literal, many answers are acceptable if they make sense. The provider needs to decide. If you are uncertain, perhaps a bit of research WITH your Learner will add enlightenment for both of you. Remember that the answers for number 2 are literal, and the answer is found right there in the text. It is possible that there are more than one answer.

Army of Frogs

3. The prey on which the frogs live would flourish, and (that ecosystem) their immediate surroundings would change.
4+. Insects would flourish, and they would destroy the vegetation. Without the plants for ground cover, the soil would dry out. The plant roots would also die, and there would be nothing to hold the soil in place. Water and wind erosion would increase. Topsoil would be moved away so crops could not be raised. Farmers would lose their ways of making a living. Wild animals would lose their protection and food sources. Any of the above answers are acceptable, and they are only suggestions.

Business of Ferrets

3. The rodent (mice and rats) population would continue to increase. Rodents would eat food needed by people and their domestic animals. Rodents also carry unhealthy germs and could increase human and animal illnesses and deaths.
4+. The predators of the ferrets would lose a large amount of their food source. The natural prey of the ferrets would increase and could cause damage to the local environment.

Colony of Seals

3. The flippers on the seals were probably used as a model from which to design wet suits that swimmers wear when they swim in deep water. Those flippers help the swimmer push against the water to move them easier and faster.
4+. Seals might become endangered if there were no laws to protect them.

Doylt of Swine

3. "I noticed that he changed the tone of his voice when he talked…"
    The other information is about the swine, and a visit to a place where swine live could prove that they *do* make those sounds.
4+. Pigs would remember where they could find food.

Embarrassment of Pandas

3. The animals are in danger of dying off so that none of that animal species is alive.
4+. Answer will completely depend on the learner's experience.

Family of Beavers

3. The beavers might have created ponds where the explorers, Lewis and Clark, could have found abundant water supply for their use. Possibilities of other answers can be determined by the provider.
4+. Some beavers might be moved, or relocated, to another habitat where their "skills" in cutting down trees might benefit their new surroundings.

Group of Guinea Pigs

In the third paragraph of the text of this animal, the activity about the weight of the animal is as follows. It was not, however, part of my suggested check for understanding.

1.5 = 1 5/10 or 1 1/2 which is the lowest common denominator. The single digit after the decimal is tenths of one whole. It does not matter IF there are numbers *before* the decimal or "dot." Only how many are *after* the decimal affect the fraction of measurement. One digit to the right, or after the decimal, is called tenths.

3. Reminder: Lay the *left* end of your ruler at the *very* first little line on the standard (inches) side of the ruler. Begin the line that you are drawing there.
4+. To solve the sleep/awake activity:
    First: 1/6 of 24. You must divide the 24 by 6=4 hours of sleep per 24 hours (one day).
    Next: 24–4=20 hours of awake time.

Horde of Hamsters

3. The answer calls for an opinion, and as long as the learner explains, to your satisfaction that is your decision.
4+. The answer should be based on thoughtful logic, and there should be an acceptable reason for that answer. They might offer some of the suggested answers to similar questions about other animals in this book.

Implausibility of Gnus

3. The gnu was probably getting a drink from a watering hole where the crocodile lived.
4+. Accept any description of climate change the learner offers. Look for information that matches about possible changes and the effects on the animals or its surroundings.

Journey of Giraffes

3. Zoos provide [patrons] affordable places to go to see and learn more about the animals that are kept there. It will help many people to become more concerned about the needs of the animals in the wild. Hopefully, that educational experience will encourage humans, of all ages, to realize the value of their existence for all of the inhabitants of this planet.

    Scientists can observe the animals to better understand needs and concerns for the protection and preservation of their species.

4+. Any time that any animal or plant becomes extinct, the balance of nature can be affected.

The suggested answers to the questions above are only examples for the provider to use to determine the accuracy of their individual learner's *thinking* skills.

More Activities for All Levels of Learners

Things to create:

- When adapted to the learners' levels, the following activities can be used. (Allow learners to do any of the preparations they can even if it doesn't look perfect.)
- Sticky notes with letters to create "word walls" for beginning readers. Learners learn from providers or more advanced learners about moving letters around on the wall to form words and simple sentences.
- Use manuscript/print.
- Write capital and lowercase alphabet letters to move around to match capital to lowercase.
- Place in alphabetical order.
- Create a consonant column and vowel column (make a few of each consonant and several of each vowel).
- Create words using the sentence strips.
- Create sentences using the sentence strips.
- Develop single syllable words, including *Mom* and *Dad*.
- Write the learner's first and last name.
- Write siblings' names.
- Use the lists of words in the spirals to post around the house where learners can see them at eye level with the learner who is trying to master them. This is great for spelling lists or content area vocabulary, formulas for math and science, social studies, etc.

Additional questions and things to do…

What does the word *hemisphere* mean? How many hemispheres does the earth have?

Compare the hemispheres to the other(s). Think about climate, size of countries found there, animals that are the same on other hemispheres, things that are different, things that are opposites…

Find the hemispheres on the atlas. Write the name of each on a separate piece of paper.

Using your atlas, find the equator. Learn about longitude and latitude.

Find the location where you live.

List the continents found in the southern hemisphere.

List the continents found in the western hemisphere.

What continents are found in more than one hemisphere?

Under the corresponding *continent* heading, write the names of the countries that were discussed in the "ABCs."

List the animals that are found on these continents.

On what continent do the fewest animals from this book exist?

Research about this continent and write a paragraph or two to explain your findings.

Under the corresponding *country*, list the animals from the "ABCs" that are found in those countries.

List the animals from the "ABCs" that are found in each hemisphere.

List the collective nouns that "make sense" after learning about the animals.

List animals according to their "general" food preference...herbivores, carnivores, omnivores, or insectivores.

List the animals that are diurnal.

List the animals that are nocturnal.

List the animals that are crepuscular.

Do additional research about any of these animals and explain their attributes that cause them to be as they are...senses that are strong or weak, tooth development, etc.

Find words within the "ABCs" that are homophones or words that sound alike but have different spellings and different meanings. An example is from the page about porcupines. The words *tale* and *tail* are homophones. List them and write their meanings, if you can determine it from their context. *Vale*, *veil*, and *vail* are other examples. List them and write them in a {rich} context of sentences. Challenge: can you use them all in the same sentence once you have learned their meanings?

Find other words that are homophones that do not necessarily have "mates" in any of my books. Add those to your vocabulary lists.

Write sentences, paragraphs, or reports about any of the things that you have learned from the use of my books. Ask your provider to do the same. Compare your writings. Who learned the most?

Categorize animals in the "ABCs" according to what kind of animal it is. Give each column a heading.

Once categorized, recategorize according to general habitat...water, air, or land.

Categorize by how many feet the animals have. Think outside the box. How many other groupings could you create?

Research the collective nouns as to culture, country, and time frame that they were introduced and used.

Find other collective nouns for these animals.

Create sentences or stories such as:

Tiger and Husker refused to run with the *pack* of ill-mannered dogs.

Maddie and Macy miss that Max is no longer part of their *mute* of dogs.

Boston is very happy to have left the *kennel* of dogs at the animal shelter, for his new-single occupancy, (canine) ever-after home.

Colt is a very gentle dog, and he enjoys opening his monthly mail delivery of special toys!

Beau is a very well-trained puppy. He even gets his own leash and takes himself for a walk. He then returns his leash to its proper place!

Create concentration games using small cards that can also be purchased in boxes of dozens. Sticky notes can also be used. Letters of the alphabet can be used for the early learners. Make two of each of the letters you intend to use. Depending on the level of development, make two capital *A*, *B*, etc. For the less experienced ones, make no more than six pairs. Increase as levels advance. You can also match a capital with its lower case.

As the levels advance, branch out into anything that you want to use as your focus: one-syllable words, words with multiple syllables; collective noun paired with its animal from the "ABCs;" academic vocabulary, etc.

Choose words from the lists you have created and see if any of them have more than one meaning. When you find any, write {rich} context sentences for each of the various meanings.

Did you find any such words as you were reading the "ABCs"? If so, how did that affect your comprehension? Watch for other such words when you are reading school assignments or your pleasure books.

Set a goal to read a new author from genre that you enjoy.

Set a goal to read a new genre written by a favorite author

For the specific kind of animals that were not listed, as kangaroo is a *marsupial* mammal, find the other animals' specific types.

When reading in leveled books, to increase fluency, set a timer with plenty of time to complete a passage. When complete accuracy is achieved at that time allotment, decrease, in small increments, the time to read the same passage. Continue doing this until speed is a maximum. Find another passage and do the same. Increase the length of the passage and continue the same pattern.

Helpful resources to expand learning to read opportunities

Some sites may require a fee. See the paragraph following entries.

- www.natgeokids.com
- Live Science >27443> zebras
- Cool Kid Facts > swan-facts-for-kids
- National Geographic
- spellzone.com
- www.pheasant.com

Some resource sites charge. Some charge after a certain number of uses, and some are in need of donations to continue offering such valuable information. I have not designated any in particular, because there are numerous reference sources that you might choose. Some sites are free. I do not know the financial capabilities of those who may compose the audience for my books. I leave that to you to decide. Please be aware of your learners' active use of the internet.

About the Author

The formal education gained during the bachelor's degree in elementary education with a reading endorsement and the master's degree in reading led Barbara to become the professional resource on whom colleagues could rely to assist in recognizing the unique needs of some of their more academically challenged students.

The high, realistic, and individualized expectations for her students in her classroom, as well as those whom she tutored, helped prepare them for future success. Her attention to requiring accountability from her students helped them to become responsible owners of their achievements.

Barbara's insightfulness has been beneficial to teachers for whom she has substitute taught. The comprehensive documentation she was able to leave as an objective and skilled professional provided valuable information. During long-term substitutions, Barbara's ability to communicate objectively and compassionately led some parents to realize the needs of their children and the role the parents could play in mitigating some of those needs.

Barbara's professional realization of the extreme needs of children and adults caused by school closures led her to write this book within a book. Her hope is that families across the United States and throughout the world will use the information and strategies in the provider section to improve the educational achievement of all learners through the application of the skills and strategies throughout the "ABCs." The "ABCs" is intentionally written as a non (leveled) book which can be used with learners from those who have no concept of print through those who read independently at the higher levels. These embedded books, once the provider has mastered the strategies in both, are intended to be a combined handbook for use with all other print for any learner.